T0171418

What Does God Want Me to Give

Dale L. Elliott

iUniverse, Inc.
Bloomington

What Does God Want Me to Give

The views expressed in this work are solely those of the author and do not necessarily reflect the views of the publisher, and the publisher hereby disclaims any responsibility for them.

iUniverse books may be ordered through booksellers or by contacting:

iUniverse
1663 Liberty Drive
Bloomington, IN 47403
www.iuniverse.com
1-800-Authors (1-800-288-4677)

Because of the dynamic nature of the Internet, any web addresses or links contained in this book may have changed since publication and may no longer be valid.

Any people depicted in stock imagery provided by Thinkstock are models, and such images are being used for illustrative purposes only.

Certain stock imagery © Thinkstock.

ISBN: 978-1-4502-7920-8 (sc)
ISBN: 978-1-4502-7921-5 (ebk)

Printed in the United States of America

iUniverse rev. date: 12/28/2010

CONTENTS

INTRODUCTION

In order to determine what God wants me to "give" you have to come to the realization of who is "my" God. You have a natural desire to be able to answer respectfully, intelligently, and more importantly truthfully. So answer the question who is "my" God?

What if you are not 100% sure about the question, what do you mean "my" God? Let me help you, answer this question.......what do you believe, deep deep down in your heart.

Who are You & What do you really believe:

1. Atheism – No real God. To really say this wouldn't you have to know 100% of everything there is to know, to make this a true statement.

2. Agnosticism –A person who holds the view that any ultimate reality (as God) is unknown and probably unknowable. It takes faith to believe in this concept, no real designer of the universe.

3. Animism - Belief in the existence of spirits separable form... spirits exist in any living creatures, such as humans mainly but also in animals.

4. Polytheism - Belief in or worship of more than one god, (golf gods, sun god, football gods)

5. Dualism - A doctrine that the universe is under the dominion of two opposing principles one of which is good and the other evil. A view of human beings as constituted of two irreducible elements (as matter and spirit).

6. Monotheism - The doctrine or belief that there is but one God, not a triune God but one and only one part God. No spirit side of God, just a male God with his own agenda.
7. Deism – Creator God can't control anything he just created the universe and watches it go…..denying the interference of the Creator with the laws of the universe.
8. Theism - belief in the existence of one God viewed as the creative source of the human race and the world who transcends yet is not in the world. Does not interact with mankind.
9. Existentialism - analysis of individual existence in an unfathomable universe and the plight of the individual who must assume ultimate responsibility for acts of free will without any certain knowledge of what is right or wrong or good or bad….Experience is God.
10. Humanism - A doctrine, attitude, or way of life centered on human interests or values; especially: a philosophy that usually rejects supernaturalism and stresses an individual's dignity and worth and capacity for self-realization through reason. Simply put "man is God".
11. Rationalism - Reliance on reason as the basis for establishment of religious truth, in other words "reason is God".
12. Materialism - A theory that physical matter is the only or fundamental reality and that all being and processes and phenomena can be explained as manifestations or results of matter.
13. Mysticism - The belief that direct knowledge of God, spiritual truth, or ultimate reality can be attained through subjective experience (as intuition or insight).
14. Monism - A view that there is only one kind of ultimate substance. The view that reality is one unitary organic whole with no independent parts, so all phenomena to one principle…matter and spirit is one.
15. Pantheism - The worship of all gods of different creeds, cults, or peoples indifferently; toleration of worship of all gods…all is God.

16. Triune Theism – One God only in three parts (Father, Son, & Holy Spirit) he created all and controls all.

So you have to answer the question each individual who is "my" God…This may be more difficult than you think.…...ask yourself what am I a slave to….work, pleasure, money…If you get down on your knees and pray "Lord God help reveal to me what it is in my life that I put above all other things on a consistent basis"……………What do I really and truly believe in. If you are still not sure and have no idea what you truly believe in and just are out there in the world hoping for the best, select the best "Triune Theism" so that you can have life, and have it more abundantly.

If you have answered the question who is my God, and you have decided to follow Jesus, then you are on the correct path. Remember this, many people will eventually come to the same decision, because the bible says All not some, not just a few, "All knees will bow, and every tongue confess Jesus Christ is Lord" (Philippians 2:10-11). It is very clear now that God's words are not vain/empty; they will come true right before your very eyes over the course of time.

Then Jesus said "if you love me keep my commandments" (John 14:15). Notice here this is in the present tense, not the past tense, nor the future tense, the *"present tense"*. He did not say you have kept, or you will start to keep…it's in the present tense. Major point if you say "Jesus" is my God, then you make a 100% commitment or surrendering to give him you're all.

Notice if you use the word commitment, while it's a really good word, who is in control when you make commitments…? The answers "You"! If you surrender, who is in control…? The Lord!

If you have decided who your God is and you made the correct choice, then keep this in your mind, "Do all things without murmurings or complaining" (Philippians 2:14)…I don't really like this one because I am so "good" at complaining, have mercy, did I see an absolute there "all" things not just some things, but "all" things……that really means to "surrender "to the Lordship of Jesus Christ and be optimistic, friendly, and joy will come upon you, not happiness, for you see happiness is only temporary, joy is for a lifetime.

1. GOD WANTS ME TO GIVE HIM...MY HEART AND MIND

1.1   HEART / CONFORM

So let's get started here.....what is the "**first**" thing God wants me to give. This is going to be answered clearly and precisely, so there is absolutely no confusion here. The first thing God wants you to give is your heart and mind to the Lord. That means you quickly come to a stopping point whatever it is your doing right now , drop to your knees and invite the Lord Jesus into your heart as Lord and Savior, believe God raised him from the dead, Jesus is the Messiah, and humbly ask for forgiveness for all your sins. You might say I have done that all ready..........when I was a little kid in grade school........do it again, right now, God has no problem with his children "reaffirming" their salvation......."know that you know"....nail this down right now.....stop and pray!

When you pick this up again realize you have surrendered your life to the Lordship of the Lord of the Universe, Jesus Christ. Give him your heart to conform it, and your mind to transform it. What in the world does that mean...?. It means for the rest of your life let the lord work from within.......you. Example right now you may not have a love for the brethren, or there may be someone in your life you say this about "Well I love um in the Lord" and never talk to or have anything to do with them. Just because you are like this today does not mean you have to be like that tomorrow. It means as long as you are alive allow the Lord to work on you from the inside out. Pray...the Lord will instill in your heart compassion *"toward people"*. This means you need to add something to your faith, what.......*"brotherly kindness"* (2nd Peter 1:7). How is "brotherly kindness" different from kindness? You see a stranger, someone you have never seen before, you show them kindness by greeting them with a warm smile and say hello when they come into your domain. Brotherly Kindness is different, if someone is your brother, you care and are concerned for their well being, dare I even say you help them *"within your means"*. Simply put, if they are struggling financially, you do not mortgage your house to help them, if you are struggling financially. God gave you a brain, so honor him by developing it. Brotherly Kindness means you take the time to get to know people. God wants you to give your heart to him, so he can work on you from within to make you more Christ like. Why should I become more Christ like and add brotherly love to my faith....? The answer is in the 11th commandment. And Jesus said "A **new commandment** I give to you, Love one another as I have loved you, that you also may love one another" (John 13:34). The badge of a Christian is love, saying "I love um in the Lord" and making it a point to never be a part of their life...is to be a part of the lie "I am who I am"......God made you and remember in some cases it takes a lifetime to make a saint. Not only can you learn, you can change your heart if you will pray about it, and here is the key..... through prayer *"TRY"* to change, and what you will find is that God will look at your heart and if you have done your part God will do his part, and you will begin to change.....I have seen this before my very eyes of people who were very hard hearted and cold and harsh, but God can do the impossible......and I believe it. You have to believe God is who he says he is, and he really can do what you may consider impossible from within you.

As you travel down life's journey remember God can work from within me, he can do the impossible, and when I look back on my life, and see how I am today, it's not the way I used to be, because I chose to allow God to work from within me. Never forget this, accept God's grace by prayerfully allowing God to conform your heart.

1.2   MIND / TRANSFORM

Transform my mind.......come on man, you gotta be kidding me, we just spoke about God changing my heart, that's good enough right?

Heart & mind they go "hand-in-hand". There is no separation here. God will transform your mind if you will let him. To have the abundant life, God wants you to have……you will need to allow God to *transform your mind*. You see it was Jesus who made it perfectly clear in John 10:10 "For the thief come not for but to steal, to kill, and to destroy, but I am come, that ye might have life, and have it more abundantly".

So how do I let God transform my mind? What does that actually mean? It means changing your mind to think the way God wants you to think.

Ok…..how do I even know what you are saying is true….? Are you telling me God himself wants me to *"think"* a certain way…? Yes, that's it…..now you're getting it….God wants you to think a certain way. Listen to what God says about what you should *"think"* about as you read his word. "Finally, brethren, whatsoever things are true, whatsoever things are honest, whatsoever things are just, whatsoever things are lovely, whatsoever things are of good report; If there be any virtue, and if there be any praise, "**think**" on these things" (Philippians 4:8). Think on these things. Wow there it is……."**think**" on these things. God does care…..what you think about.

1.3 CONVERSATION

Another things God wants you to think about is "what you say to others". No hold on here just a minute…..God actually cares about what I say to other people……even in…….idle conversation……come-on, man you gotta be kidding me right? No I am not kidding you, God does care about "all" of your conversation even your idle conversation. "But I say unto you, every idle word that men shall speak, they shall give account therefore in the day of judgment" (Matthew 12:36). Have mercy I can't even remember some of the idle words I have spoken…… how should I speak when I am not using idle words……I mean does God care about my normal conversation….? "But as he which hath called you is holy, so be ye holy in **all** manner of conversation; because it is written, be ye holy, for I am holy". (1ˢᵗ Peter 1:15). So here God is saying be ye holy in **all** manner of conversation. Transform you mind to think along these lines of controlling your speech & language and what comes out of your mouth is not guile. Guile what in the world does that word mean…? Guile means deceitful, cunning, with some harmful intent to others. Ok, ok, so you are saying……God actually wants me to transform my mind to the point of…what I think about, and what I actually say in my everyday speech. Yes…If you want to love life, and want to see good days. Everybody wants to love life and see good days right, what does that have to do with what I say. "For he that will love life, and see good days, let him refrain his tongue from evil, and his lips that they speak no guile: Let him eschew evil, and do good; let him seek peace, and ensue it" (1st Peter 3:10-11). So God wants you to transform you mind and speak no evil from your lips, in fact he wants you to eschew-(meaning to avoid habitually) evil with your speech/language. God wants you to think on things that are lovely.

What about that part you spoke about earlier where you said think on things that are lovely……Women are lovely! It's alright to think about "*lovely women*" correct? Here is how God wants you to transform your mind concerning women. 1st Peter 4:1-2 "For as much then as Christ hath suffered for us in the flesh, are yourselves likewise with the same **mind**: for he that hath suffered in the flesh hath ceased from sin: that he no longer should live the rest of his time in the flesh to the lusts of men, but to the will of God.". This means you should not "lust" after women. Hear the words of God as Jesus says in Matthew 5:28 "But I say unto you, That whosoever looketh on a woman to lust after her hath committed adultery with her already in his heart". God is saying transform you mind when you look at women do not have elevator eyes and check them out from top to bottom…nor have sexual thoughts about them in your mind. God is saying transform your mind, here. Peter gives an example listen to this:

"But chiefly them that walk after the flesh in the lust of uncleanness, and despise government. Presumptuous are they, self-willed, they are not afraid to speak evil of dignities. But these, as natural brute beasts, made to be taken and destroyed, speak evil of the things that they understand not; and shall utterly perish in their own corruption; and shall receive the reward of unrighteousness,. as they that count it pleasure to riot in the day time. Spots they are and blemishes, sporting themselves with their own deceiving while they feast with you; having eyes full of adultery, and that cannot cease from sin; beguiling unstable souls: an heart they have exercised with covetous practices; cursed children: which have forsaken the right way, and are gone astray, following the way of idols, who loved the wages of the unrighteousness;" (2ⁿᵈ Peter 2:10, 12-15).........God is saying......see the mind of the unrighteousness.........transform your mind, to righteousness, by eliminating "lust", thinking on things that are true, honest, just, pure, lovely, and come under good report. There is a lost art among all Christians today, and that is the art of "meditation". You mean God wants to transform my mind by having me thinking or rather meditating upon certain thoughts. Yes, God wants to transform your mind if you will......of your own free will and accord accept God's grace and let him help you......by meditating or thinking about God's words.......check out the following:

- "Psalms 1 Blessed is the man.......his delight is in the law of the lord; and in his law doth he **meditate** day and night."

- "Joshua 1:8 This book of the law shall not depart out of thy mouth; but thou shalt **meditate** therein day and night, that thou mayest observe to do according to all that is written therein: for then thou shalt make thy way prosperous, and then thou shalt have good success.

- "Psalms 119:15 I will **meditate** in thy precepts, and have respect unto thy ways".

- "Psalms 119:148 Mine eyes prevent the [night] watches, that I might **meditate** in thy word".

- "Psalms 143:5 I remember the days of old; I **meditate** on all thy works; I muse on the work of thy hands".

1.4   MIND / THE CHANGES COMES FROM WITHIN

This is how God will transform your mind if you will allow God to change you from within. You see God wants you to give your heart and your mind to him, just like when you got saved, so he can truly change you as you travel down life's journey. Do not, I repeat do not, listen to the lie.....I cannot learn, I cannot improve or work on anything in my spiritual life.......I am who I am , this is how God made me.....well God gave you.....your own free will and accord to either grow and do the right thing and allow God to work with you all your life.........or of your own free will and accord not grow and accept the worldly lie of "this is who God made me", and I can't change who I am…(**LIE**)!!!

When you're green you grow, and when you're not you rot……. think about it.

Some of you would like to stop the process……I want to be a certain weight and never loose or gain any more, a certain height and never grow or shrink, my hair grows to a certain length and never grows any more, my beard grows to a certain length and stops, my hair stays a certain color and never changes to gray or falls out…….my skin gets to a certain texture and never ages, the weather never changes it's all about 65 degrees and sunny with a few clouds, the seasons never change……….Do you think God likes change. Yes God, likes for **you** to change from within, so let God work in your life, let God change your heart and mind.

"Romans 12:2 And be not **conformed** to this world, but be ye **transformed** by the renewing of your mind, that ye may prove what is that good, and acceptable, and the perfect will of God."

God wants you to give him…….your heart and mind to be conformed and transformed to his walk in his way!

2. GOD WANTS ME TO GIVE MONEY

2.1 TOTALLY FALSE ASSUMPTIONS

2. 1 -God is happy and *totally* pleased with me if all I do is go to church every now and then and tithe, you know like a dollar or "*maybe*" five dollars in the offering plate. (fill a pew) Not True

2. 2 -God does not want my best, he wants my "left -over's". In other words If we get a new couch for the den, well I can take my "old-worn-out" aka "*left-over*" couch and give it to the church. Not True

2. 3 -I should only tithe If can get some personal benefit out of it. Not True

2. 4 -I can totally erase/ignore that part in the book of Malachi where it says "offerings"…you know the part is says tithes and offerings… ..I don't like the offerings part, so I can just ignore that part. Come on dude, I give 10% off "gross income," get off my back already, God does not want anything else from me. Not True

2. 5 -If I tithe, I should have some "*say-so*" on how things are run in church, after all it's my money paying for the preacher salary, therefore he should do things "**my-way**". Not True

2. 6 -Tithe money should only be spent on the utility bills and the bare minimum expenses necessary for the staff and preacher, after all they don't really work. Not True. .

2. 7 -If I tithe God should hear my prayers above others based on the dollar amount of the tithe, so he who tithes the most should receive a priority to answering prayers correct...? Not True

2. 8 -Biggest lie of all.........I cannot afford to tithe, you see I don't make much money. Not True. Biggest lie of all.........I cannot tithe, you see I make too much money (millions of dollars). Not True.

2.2 TITHE & JUST GO TO CHRUCH IT'S ALL GOOD RIGHT?

- God is happy and *totally* pleased with me if all I do is go to church every now and then and tithe, you know like a dollar or *"maybe"* five dollars in the offering plate. (fill a pew) Not True

God is **not** happy with you because you have just decided to disobey his word, or you have no knowledge of his word, or you do have knowledge of his word and totally decide you should be the one, not God.......but you decides on how much, if any, that you will or will not tithe. God's word is crystal clear on this one, "*you*" do not decide how much to tithe. It clearly says in "Leviticus 27:32 And concerning the **tithe** of the herd, or of the flock, [even] of whatsoever passeth under the rod, the **tenth** shall be holy unto the LORD" and here again in "Numbers 18:26 . Thus speak unto the Levites, and say unto them, when ye take of the children of Israel the tithes which I have given you from them for your inheritance, then ye shall offer up an heave offering of it for the LORD, [even] a **tenth** [part] of the tithe."

So understand this If your place of business met once a week and everyone who worked there gave a dollar or 5 dollars could this pay for all of your expenses....no of course not.....thus to operate a church it takes more than a dollar. God wants you to give 10% of the gross part of your income.

Now wait just a minute here man, I don't get gross I only get net, if it's good enough for me why it that not good enough for God, after all that is all I get....? The bible is clear again here......on the first fruits you bring the first fruits, to God listen to scripture.....2nd Chronicles 31:5 And as soon as the commandment came abroad, the children of Israel brought in abundance the first fruits of corn, wine, and oil, and honey, and of **all** the increase of the field; and the tithe of all [things] brought they in abundantly. God takes everything into account and reads you heart and mind when you tithe......and God warns you about making your own decisions about these issues.....listen "Titus 1:14 Not giving heed to Jewish fables, and commandments of men, that turn from the truth.

Then listen to the messiah here:

"Mark 12:41-44 And there came a certain poor widow, and she threw in two mites, which make a farthing, And he called [unto him] his disciples, and saith unto them, Verily I say unto you, That this poor widow hath cast more in, than all they which have cast into the treasury: For all [they] did cast in of their abundance; but she of her want did cast in all that she had, [even] all her living." .

Notice Jesus reads the **heart** and the **mind** and he knows why & how "**you**" tithe. He truly understand the motives behind why you tithe.

2.3   LEFT OVERS IT'S ALL GOOD RIGHT?

- God does not want my best, he wants my "left -over's". In other words If we get a new couch for the den, well I can take my "old-worn-out" aka "*left-over*" couch and give it to the church. Not True

So many times we get this wrong. It is amazing, that you should look at God's house here on the planet earth and think, thoughts like.....my children do not play with their baby toys.....why don't I donate them to the church.......then you do this and actually feel good about yourself, some of you even get "*rotator cuff injuries*" patting yourselves on the back.

God did not say bring me...whatever is worthless to you, and if it's just taking up space and clutter in your house let me have it. This is God's house and should be treated with the utmost respect. Remember people used to die when they went into the holy of holies......if their hearts and minds were not properly prepared, or they did not follow the instructions God gave the priest. This is a big deal......do not go the way of "Cain".

Here is what God did say about the first fruits:

Exodus 22:29 Thou shalt not delay [to offer] the first of thy ripe fruits, and of thy liquors: the firstborn of thy sons shalt thou give unto me". Again in…."Nehemiah 10:35 And to bring the firstfruits of our ground, and the firstfruits of all fruit of all trees, year by year, unto the house of the LORD:"……notice here the ground work you do……the very best you have to offer you bring to the Lord! Whatever type of income that comes into your life…….give the first 10% to God, and God will honor this.

Some of you want to argue at this point and say **if** I "*did not donate*", then the church would not have "**anything**" for the poor little children to play with. And perhaps you are one of these rare people who have kept the toys in "mint" condition, and done nothing but try to enhance the life of the "*other little kids*" that will visit the church in the future. But you see God requires the "**First Fruits**", and he wants you to give with all of your heart and mind, not just an "**after thought**" of getting rid of what you consider to be junk concerning your immediate family needs. Listen once again about the first fruits: "2nd Chronicles 31:5 And as soon as the commandment came abroad, the children of Israel brought in abundance the **first fruits** of corn, wine, and oil, and honey, and of **all** the increase of the field; and the tithe of all [things] brought they in abundantly".

Listen to the Lord Jesus:

"Luke 11:42 But woe unto you, Pharisees! for ye **tithe** mint and rue and all manner of herbs, and pass over judgment and the love of God: these ought ye to have done, and not to leave the other undone".

So simply put God does not want your "**left-over's**", if you see a need for the church, perhaps you should make this a ministry of yours and shop around if though you were buying for your own family, and purchase the latest and greats items. Even if you have to save up "*a little at a time*" to make the best choice, then when you stand before God, you receive the reward God desires to give you because you held true to the scriptures and brought your best and first fruits to the Lord God Almighty. Your intentions is to honor and glorify god with your best…….God clearly sees your heart and mind, God knows your motive, intention, the how & why……..Allow God to reward you to the best of your abilities, nothing less than 100%. Perhaps you have read this once upon a time "Matthew 6: 20-21 But lay up for yourselves treasures in heaven, where neither moth nor rust doth corrupt, and where thieves do not break through nor steal: For where your treasure is, there will your heart be also".

You may have thought, how on earth do I…lay up treasures in heaven for myself…..the aforementioned example is how……you follow God's commandments…….will all your heart, mind, and strength (actions).

2.4　Tithe or Give "only" If I get something out of it right?

- I should only tithe If can get some personal benefit out of it. Not True

I wish I could tell you I have never thought this way, or viewed tithe, in this perspective. Unfortunately we all have entertained thoughts along this line. Human nature is to use currency to receive something of immediate or future value to us. And usually our future is relatively "short term" along with our patience. The idea that we should *"trust"* God…..and step out on "Faith"…..come on now that's…….well that goes against everything we learned in school. This does not add up on paper, nor does this seem beneficial to my income statement……..Oh yeah right……Faith…..trust God? Please listen to this very closely God actually says……one place in the bible God says *"test me"* on this…… .."Malachi 3:11 Bring ye all the tithes into the storehouse, that there may be meat in mine house, and **prove me now herewith**, saith the LORD of hosts, if I will not open you the windows of heaven, and pour you out a blessing, that [there shall] not [be room] enough [to receive it]. You can test God on this one, what you will find is that if you tithe with the right heart and mind……not for a personal gratification, but because you "love the lord" and have *faith* & *trust him*………..Pray this prayer from proverbs every time you have a tithe check in your hand. "Proverbs 3:5 Dear Lord I claim this scripture even though I don't fully understand how tithe works……Trust in the LORD with all thine heart; and lean not unto thine own understanding.

Guess what will happen if you tithe with the right heart & mind, God will open doors you can't imagine, everyone is laid off but "you"…….

you move on to a much better job, a situation.......or a situation with your spouse, son or daughter is suddenly resolved.....it's amazing to see how God works in each and every individual life of those who truly "love him" & trust him. The central core truth is.....you *"can't"* afford **not** to tithe.

God wants you to give 10% of your first fruits to him.......gross income.....*any* income God puts in your life.

2.5 I can ignore or Erase that part about OFFERINGS RIGHT?

- I can totally erase/ignore that part in the book of Malachi where it says "offerings"...you know the part it says tithes and offerings.....I don't like the offerings part, so I can just ignore that part. Come on dude, I give 10% off "gross income," get off my back already, God does not want anything else from me. Not True

So many times I see the people losing out on blessings because of the wrong attitude. Showing up for Church & Sunday school, even tithing 10% of gross income and going home. Never involved in their church really, unless some church function is offsite like a "Men's Spring Golf Tournament", or a "Ladies Spa Day", or something where they are offsite doing something **me myself** and **I** like to do, but totally having no part in the section entitled "offerings" You may be familiar with Malachi 3:8 where God spells it out for you:

> "Malachi 3:8 Will a man rob God? Yet ye have robbed me. But ye say, Wherein have we robbed thee? In tithes and offerings. Ye [are] cursed with a curse: for ye have robbed me, [even] this whole nation. Bring ye all the tithes into the storehouse, that there may be meat in mine house, and prove me now herewith, saith the LORD of hosts, if I will not open you the windows of heaven, and pour you out a blessing, that [there shall] not [be room] enough [to receive it]".

Let's define **tithe**: *A tithe means ten percent of **all** benefits that come our way, like, our salary, any kind of inheritance(s), all gifts, findings, fees, tips, and interest earned on financial transactions/ accounts, or any consideration made available to you, under the entire canopy of heaven.*

Let's define ***offering***: *The offerings given unto the Lord God has to be over and above your ten percent tithe; after tithe, now you can give your offering…..as God is leading you to do so………by the holy spirit of God……as to specific need(s),presented to you……they may be in the form of service, volunteer work, or sharing of your talents….in areas of ministry where God opens the door of opportunity for you. I would consider prayer as an essential ingredient concerning offerings.*

What……tithe and offerings are the same thing right…..? No they are not the same thing. First notice they are mention, (tithes and offerings), in the same sentence. God did this for a reason. So what in the world is…."Offerings". Let's seek God wisdom and find the answer. I am not a CPA, but I have worked in and around accounting most of my career, and I have a B.A. degree in "accounting", when I got involved in my church they actually "ask" me to be a part of the counting committee, having no knowledge I had "any" accounting experiences whatsoever…….see how God works in your life if you will only let him. What's a counting committee? That is counting the tithe money at the end of the services and balancing the books (you have to know a little about accounting, not a lot) and this was the way I could bring my firstfruits…..aka……my God given talents and give back or share my talents to serve.

So God wants you to give "offering(**s**)", and bring to him your talents and abilities to serve him as an offering. Some of you may say, what can I do……I can't teach, preach, or sing…...I assure you God has given all of us talents……..I want to say let's read 1ˢᵗ Corinthians chapter 12, but I will point out one verse that is especially worth noting here and that is verse 11. "1ˢᵗ Corinthians 12:11 But all these worketh that one and the selfsame Spirit, dividing to every man severally as he will". Notice here that what God is saying you are given more than one talent. Use your God given talents to be used as offerings of service to the Lord. Sometimes your God given talents are…..making money…… raising money……use these to serve the Lord. There is always a project of some sort on the horizon if only we could raise enough money for it……….? Each of our gifts are different, some can cook…..did you say cook…why yes…..then by all means help the church with fellowships, when some ones family members die…..etc………..Get plugged in your own church and use your talents to serve the Lord.

"Romans 12:6 Having then gift(**s**), then differing according to the grace…….have you notice the word is plural and we are given more than one gift.

I have also been able to accept the grace and mercy of God by circumstances……being able to teach Co-Teach Sunday School at my local church. Let me tell you this, if you had told me years ago I would move to Tallahassee FL, and co-teach "adults" Sunday School every Sunday………I would have been fleeing like Jonah…..It would have sacred me to death……Why *"my own personal lack of faith"* I listened to the Lie "you're not qualified, you're not able to do this, you don't have the credentials, you're not equipped to do this"……….but when I trusted in God, he equipped me, provided for me, and guided me, in the way he can that puts asunder all the worldly excuses. What does this have to do with you……the point is you have several talents God has equipped you with…….to serve him, and they are different for each of us, maybe it is just to discover what God has equipped you with…… how do you do that……find out your talents God has given you to serve the body aka church aka to serve God with your own personal offerings….?.

- First here is what you do, *"Go to the Lord in Prayer about it"* ask God to help reveal to you…….your God given talents he has given you to serve him…….help you to come to realization of what they are.

- Second ask yourself these questions:

  - What am I good at?

  - What do I enjoy doing?

  - Has the Holy Spirit given me peace about what God has called me to do?

  - Do I encourage others to help build the body of Christ?

Simple put God wants you to give an offering......your firstfruits – tithe 1st and beyond this an offerings.......Please don't forfeit any heavenly rewards......serve the Lord with your talents, and discover a new and wonderful blessing the Lord will provide!.

2.6   MY MONEY I HAVE A SAY IN HOW IT'S SPENT RIGHT?

* If I tithe, I should have some "*say-so*" on how things are run in church, after all it's my money paying for the preacher salary; therefore he should do things "**my-way**". Not True

Tithe should be spent on utilities and the "bare" minimum expenses for just the preacher and his salary. They "*church staff*" don't really need to make out a budget; after all it's really simple, and the church does not need internet this is not what I want to be paying for in my tithe money, and do they really need any type of retirement plans for "preachers" or "associate pastors", or "youth ministers". I mean come on.......they don't really work, you know what I mean by that right, they do not have a set schedule (8AM-5PM), accountability, really they only have to prepare for Sunday and there done right?

A lot of people don't realize that an entire world is happening in their own church requiring lots or preparation and work with "*Sunday Mornings*" being the most visible part of the church. If you have ever worked and actually gotten involved in your church and taken any responsibility role.......in a program such as "Vacation Bible School", Preparing the weekly bulletin, scheduling a calendar of events during the summer for just one department (like the Senior Adults) or directing the summer camp for children, or Judgment House (walk through drama big production) , or Good News Club, or a Men's Retreat, or a Lady's retreat, or a Sunday night food fellowship, you realize all the money and work involved to actually pull this off successfully without running out of supplies, air conditioning, heating, workers, or patience.....then you understand this is a project of its own. So this begs the question of well I tithe, therefore I should have a "*say-so*" of how we spend the money. A budget is a fundamental necessity all churches make and usually adhere to very well. Should you have a say on how the church is governed, are you on any active committee in your church? if not ask the "*nominating committee*" to recommend you next time, but more importantly get a copy of the budget and follow it closely, and monitor your own church's progress and see if they are going way over or under in the category of "miscellaneous" and judge the budget for yourself. If you have credentials like a major in accounting or finance or you prepare budgets every day in your job and monitor them and stick to them, then please get involved in your church and ask your pastors, how may I serve, here are my qualifying credentials. The answer here is maybe you should have a "say-so" and you can add value to your church by serving on a committee or in some capacity but go through the proper protocol and get involved.

Understand this point very clearly, God entrust the government of the church to the "Pastor" and unless he is ***incapacitated*** (there has been cases of misconduct & fraud that's why the pastor should be carefully chosen and "*internal controls*" in place) we should be submissive to his authority, and from a spiritual perspective God should always be consulted prior to us "*changing anything in our church*". What do you mean here…?

God **always** has a plan, and within this plan be aware there are two parts here.

1st God's perfect will (God's way that is perfect) and achieves the plan flawlessly.

2nd God's permissive will (God's can allow his will to be accomplished by other routes)

God will have……."his will"…….done either by Route A, or Route B, but either way God's will is going to be accomplished, but through the prayers of his people he may allow a different route to be taken that still accomplishes God's will. (Permissive Will). So tread lightly here make sure you are in the will of God and understand what is at stake when you pray.

What did you mean by internal controls…….anyone who went to college and took an accounting class this was hammered home……. but even without a degree everyone knows…….. you don't let the fox watch the hen house. Simple put there should be a finance committee overseeing the budget is adhered to……and….an outside audit done every year by an independent non-affiliated company to closely monitor the appropriations accordingly.

People in the congregation have talents, use them. In a small church of 300 I know at least (3) CPA's who could be in charge of setting up and hiring an external auditor. If your church cannot afford it (1ˢᵗ red flag goes up here) then use the men & women of the congregation who have talents and abilities in auditing and let them do an internal audit, reporting to a independent church counsel group or board. To be good stewards we should take *"many"* internal control measures other than the major ones I listed here. Example how the offering plates are collect after they have been passed around, how they get from the back to the *"counters"* (people who count the money). There should be a safe installed, the financial officer should oversee this with a different deacon every week never the same people every week. You need different accounting people counting each month or quarter(s) or if you have the staff.......different counters each week. The main point here is the pastor should not be the one collecting all the money, counting all the money, and making the deposit in the bank---

That's nice now back to **me, myself**, and...**I**.............."I" should have a say in what & how our money is spent correct. The church is self governed. You need to make out a financial plan with an actual budget and a visionary budget. Now wait a second here I should just *"give a command"* and the congregation and especially the preacher should follow *"my command"*, after all I am the CEO of a very successfully company, and we made a hefty profit last year (don't tell the IRS that) under my leadership. That's where the visionary budget comes into play. With a budget you know historically what the basic necessity expenses are and you should know what it takes each week to stay above red. Here is how it should be laid out:

Operational Budget – This is your utilities expense and are unavoidable, also many items in this category should be review regularly like office supplies, envelopes, bulletin expenses, normal maintenance and repairs. Depending on the size of the church this can be vast or small. If the church is big enough you should have an audit committee doing research to see if there is a way mitigate the cost, like we are getting our insurance from "Company-"A" can another insurance company provide a better rate.......we are and always have been doing business this way with this company.......well then someone should make a few phone calls and see if their rates are low, medium or high comparatively.

One item of great debate here is a *"Visionary Budget"* side-by-side the Operational Budget. What is that…? A *"Visionary Budget"* is set aside funds for projects. Example you may have an idea for a project like a "Trip to Brazil" to build a church, this is good idea, but will the church have the necessary funds to pay for this project, and what about **all** the **other good ideas**? There needs to be a process involved where the church list the Visionary Budget alphabetically and then the church reviews the list, **votes** on the "priority" of each item on the list and ranks all items on the "Visionary Budget" accordingly. Then over time as funds are allocated (saved up) for a particular project the church can say ok now after Two years we have enough funds for the Visionary Budget *"Trip to Brazil"* to build a church, and so if you are interested in going this how much money you will need to raise personally to pay for (passport, airline, hotel, food, etc.…). So herein lies the debate….. some say all money goes to the operational budget, and only what is left over goes to the Visionary Budget and no one should be able to fill out an envelope saying I want to give 100 tithe and 100 to *"Trip to Brazil"*……..Or just the opposite if we give money and spec out the necessary set aside funds, then eventually over time we can reach the goal.

After reading the aforementioned process of Operational Budget and Visionary Budget do you have an opinion? If you do please for the love of God, get involved in your own church. I am a firm believer that all the tithes and set aside funds are put where they are intended to go……then you ask the question this is what we need this week to meet our basic operational needs, did we collect the minimum and meet that goal, if not then we have to subtract from the set aside funds to meet the minimum operation expenses. If we did meet the minimum then **all** the other funds go to the set aside funds as "specified out" in the tithe envelopes.

Back to **Me**, **Myself**, and **I**……this is where church splits and you miss out on blessing the Lord has in store for you. If you as a church family vote on the list of items in the Visionary Budget, and your own personal wishes do not meet the list in the order you wanted them too…….people get really bent out of shape. Example you personally feel

the "*Trip to Brazil*" should be 3rd on the list and say after the church voted it came in 7th on the list of priorities. Believe it or not some people say I don't want to be a part of this church anymore.....totally forgetting God, and very selfishly focusing on **Me**, **Myself**, and **I**.........
You should be at church to worship and learn about God....this budget stuff you should be willing to vote-on, and accept as a church family....
and support one another.

One last item worth mentioning here is there should be a process by which items make it to the "Visionary Budget". In other words, say I have an idea we go to the remote outskirts of "Viet Nam" and witness to the people in the villages. Maybe this item should never make it to the "Visionary Budget"......why not? It cost each individual about $10,000 a piece, the people do not speak English, we have no interpreter, and eating the wrong food could cause the entire group to get very sick, only (2) people are interested in doing this church wide, and perhaps its an overall "**ineffective**" ministry. Clearly there should be some guidelines on what projects make the "Visionary Budget".

- Business Rule 1   The project has to bring glory to God, there must be some approval process.

- Business Rule 2   You have to be 21 or older to submit project proposals.

- Business Rule 3   The cost is reasonable & obtainable within a certain time period.

- Business Rule 4   Re-submittals projects will be documented and are up for "re-submittal" (example it violates one of the other rules....send youth to Hawaii to gamble) No....refine it they go to Hawaii to witness to others...very structured outreach ministry, and very organized on when, where, & how....etc...

2.7   THE RICH GET PRIORITY TREATMENT

- If I tithe God should hear my prayers above others based on the dollar amount of the tithe, so he who tithes the most

should receive a priority to answering prayers correct...?
Not True

This is probably the way a lot of people think, even though they may not admit it. Most people think, If I give more, God can be more susceptible to "*hearing / answering*" my prayers. Before I can say anything here I have to mention this one important and critical part of scripture. It is one of my favorites too: ISAIAH 55:8-9 "For my thoughts [are] not your thoughts, neither [are] your ways my ways, saith the LORD. For [as] the heavens are higher than the earth, so are my ways higher than your ways, and my thoughts than your thoughts".

This means God does not think like mankind thinks. His thoughts are higher than our thoughts after all he has no need of money, and he is both "inside" & "outside" of time as we know it. Everything the human being does is a project. Simply put your whole life is from one project to the next. A project being defined as something with a start date, end date, and goal you would like to get achieve. Some projects you do every day.......Project 1 get ready for work alarm goes off at 5:00-Project start time.......hit snooze until 5:30, get up at 5:30 shave, shower, dress, prepare, breakfast "*coffee or meal*", then leave the house at 6:30-Project end time........In other words everything humans do has:

[a...start date/start time........target/goal........end date/end time.] God does not operate in this realm.........of the human calendar & time. Time is not a factor for him, as it is for us. Reality is we are on "God's Calendar & Time Schedule"........we do not have access to this nor do we need access to this............it would just worry us to no end if we even glimpsed a section of it.......God is good, all the time. So let's think about this.......God created us, he does not need money, he operates in the realm of time as he chooses, he has all that he can desire or not desire.........where do you and I come in with our tithes and offerings. God has all the robots he wants they are called angels.....they can see him there is not a question of "does God exist".......they see him, he can destroy and create new ones accordingly as he chooses.......then why does he care about me and what I give...? We are his masterpieces' that's why. We the human beings are created in God's image......wow what an honor and privilege this is.......being created in God's image. Do not take it lightly; God has a desire that we would, unlike the angles......of our own free will and accord, choose for ourselves to accept him, and believe in him having no visual verification of him....but believe "having Faith in his word" . God's intent on this issue has been debated though the centuries about this one single incident, but closely follow his words here: 2nd Peter 3:9 The Lord is not slack concerning his promise, as some **men** count slackness; but is longsuffering to us-ward, not willing that any **should perish**, but that **all should** come to repentance. You see the intent of God is that all, not some, but all mankind come to repentance and realize we need God, and to come to him in "faith" without seeing him, but having faith he is there and God is who he says he is........and depending on him in our "daily" lives.

Just because you give one dollar or one million dollars is not important, you get no special privileges based on dollar amount. Why....God's word....listen here: "Romans 12: 3 For I say, through the grace given unto me, to every man that is among you, not to think [of himself] more highly than he ought to think; but to think soberly, according as God hath dealt to every man the measure of faith".

You see God tells us over and over and over again........the one thing he as the creator has that no creature aka mankind does not have is the ability to read the heart and mind. God has this ability and human beings do not have this ability. How on earth do you know God has this ability then.....? Mark 12:41-44 "And Jesus sat over against the treasury, and beheld how the people cast money into the treasury: and many that were rich cast in much. And he called [unto him] his disciples, and saith unto them, Verily I say unto you, That this poor widow hath cast more in, than all they which have cast into the treasury: For all [they] did cast in of their abundance; but she of her want did cast in all that she had, [even] all her living.

Jesus had never spoken to the widow before, nor had he known her, yet he could read the heart and mind of the individual. Jesus is God.... John 10:30 "**I and [my] Father are one**".

The amount you give is important, God will judge you on how and why and what your motive to give is.........think about it.........God reads you heart and mind crystal clearly, without error.......a safety feature he built in as a way of dealing with mankind............think about this.......next time you give any amount.....do you love the Lord thy God...? What is your motive for giving?

God wants you to give 10% of your first fruits according to your means. Giving beyond that is between you and God and should be carefully prayed over, and no amount given beyond 10% until God lays on your heart what amount to give according to your own individual means.

2.8   You can't afford not to Tithe

- Biggest lie of all part A.........I cannot afford to tithe, you see I don't make much money. Not True.

- Biggest lie of all part B.........I cannot tithe, you see I make too much money (Millions of Dollars). Not True

1st of all if you think for a single minute any part of the part A or part B statement(s) are true, please, go back and read all of chapter two three times then pick up again here.

This will be very brief. Give 10% of your gross income to God, at the church you attend, and read this verse of scripture over and over and over again, mediate upon it until you know it backwards and forwards, and you really understand it. Proverbs 3:5-6 "Trust in the LORD with all thine heart; and lean not unto thine own understanding. In all thy ways acknowledge him, and **he** shall direct thy paths".

If you really make too much money......remember God has blessed you with the ability to acquire the wealth, and just as easily as you have obtained it God can take it from you........heart attack, stroke, deadly diseases, accidents..........it has been said by greater men then me all human beings are about one decision away from stupid.......meaning we can all make mistakes that cost us dearly. Your empire can be taken from you......God is a great and a merciful God, but there is a side to him.......the *"Wrath of God"* we do not like to discuss and sometimes God will do whatever it takes to get your attention........life and death are in his hands and God decides what you acquire and what you don't acquire here on this earth........believe it or not God is in control. Remember you are blessed in the fact God gave you the ability to build/acquire.......an empire; he wants you to use it to bring glory to his name. So bring glory and honor to God by being a good steward of what God has blessed you with......the ability to acquire wealth, you may think I did this on my own......Believe me God has blessed you with this ability.........now honor God and bring glory to his name.

What if you barley make enough to live on.....you will go into negative numbers or supersede the expensive category if you tithe.......I would strongly encourage you to examine the budget, **tithe anyway** even though it does not work out on paper, and then trust God to help you make it. You will be amazed and find it hard to believe but God will help you make it. I know I have been in this category most of my life and God has always been faithful even when I thought it was physically impossible. Recently, I accumulated many medical bills, and thought ok God there is no way I can get out of this financial pit.......how on earth am I going to survive. My own church family stepped up and helped me with my medical bills (I did not even ask for help), and the tears I cried humbled me and brought me to my knees praising God and thanking him for doing the impossible again within my own life. God is Good, All the Time!

God wants you to give 10% of your first fruits according to your means. Giving according to your own individual means........is started with a logical 10% of gross income and giving because you Love the Lord thy God with all your heart, mind, soul, and strength. And by Strength we mean our actions.....this shows the love we have for God.

Simply put no matter what income level you are at.....You cannot afford not to tithe!

3. God wants me to give Faithfulness

3.1 Faithfulness to worship God

What do you mean here, God actually wants me to give him my own personal faithfulness to worship him? Yes once you become a Christian God wants you to mature and grow along the way not sit… idly by and watch the "*show*" ……..sorta-speak. Do not just fill a pew or seat……. God wants you to become an active participant in the worship service. How do you do that, the 1st step is to prepare your heart and mind to come into the Lord's house. This is done with a great respect for who God is and a growing faith in allowing God to work in your life. Where in the holy scriptures does he say he wants faithfulness. 1st Corinthians 1:9 God [is] faithful, by whom ye were called unto the fellowship of his Son Jesus Christ our Lord. Look at 1st Corinthians 4:1-2 Let a man so account of us, as of the ministers of Christ, and stewards of the mysteries of God. Moreover it is required in stewards, that a man be found faithful. So you see you are required and ask to be a good steward and be faithful, so you can grow in grace and knowledge of our Lord Jesus Christ. This means you should faithfully attend the worship services and take it ever so seriously pray before you enter the sanctuary this prayer:

1. God if there a biblical truth in my life you need to reveal to me, open up my heart and mind to receive it.

2. God help me to take the interpretation of the biblical truth and apply it to my life.
3. God help me to have "Faith" in my heart and mind "***deeply rooted***" in the word of God.

God wants you to give him your faithfulness.

3.2 FAITHFULNESS TO TEMPTATIONS

This is good and true and but what about faithfulness in those times when I am tempted the most. 1st Corinthians 10:13 There hath no temptation taken you but such as is common to man: but God [is] faithful, who will not suffer you to be tempted above that ye are able; but will with the temptation also make a way to escape, that ye may be able to bear [it]. Remember when the 1st Jew ever…….Abraham was tested by God what Abraham did. He got up early in the morning, prepared, and set out on the task ahead of him, he did not linger, have a committee meeting, or debate the matter long, he did what God told him to do…….without hesitation/deviating. Galatians 3:9 So then they which be of faith are blessed with **faithful** Abraham. And also in 1st Thessalonians 5:23-24 And the very God of peace sanctify you wholly; and [I pray God] your whole spirit and soul and body be preserved blameless unto the coming of our Lord Jesus Christ. Faithful [is] he that calleth you, who also will do [it].

So you can see that you are called to be faithful, and this helps you in your daily walk with God.

So what can you lean about temptations and the faithfulness it takes to combat this: The answer lies within the precious book of James: listen to the holy scriptures as we travel down life's journey. I strongly suggest you highlight underline or make a mental note of the words given in reference to scripture:

James 1:12Blessed [is] the man that endureth temptation: for when he is tried, he shall receive the crown of life, which the Lord hath promised to them that love him. James 1:13 Let no man say when he is tempted, I am tempted of God: for God cannot be tempted with evil, neither tempteth he any man: James 1:14 But every man is tempted, when he is drawn away of his own lust, and enticed. James 1:15 Then when lust hath conceived, it bringeth forth sin: and sin, when it is finished, bringeth forth death. James 1:16 Do not err, my beloved brethren. James 1:17 Every good gift and every perfect gift is from above, and cometh down from the Father of lights, with whom is no variableness, neither shadow of turning. James 1:18 Of his own will begat he us with the word of truth, that we should be a kind of firstfruits of his creatures. James 1:19 ¶ Wherefore, my beloved brethren, let every man be swift to hear, slow to speak, slow to wrath: James 1:20 For the wrath of man worketh not the righteousness of God. James 1:21 ¶ Wherefore lay apart all filthiness and superfluity of naughtiness, and receive with meekness the engrafted word, which is able to save your souls. James 1:22 But be ye doers of the word, and not hearers only, deceiving your own selves.

This is why being faithful is so important; the walk of maturity in Christian faith is laborious in that it requires work and action on your part. It not a simple one line *"fix all"* type of philosophy, what you are tempted in…….and what I am tempted in…….are completely different.

3.3 LEVEL OF FAITHFULNESS DEFINED BY A DECIMAL POINT

Is the level of your faithfulness to God's word directly portioned to a decimal point? Even to the point of destroying your witness? Here is what I am talking about, say you go in to buy an item you have saved up money for……..say for a long period of time. When you make the payment, and walk out of the store you are sitting in your car looking over the receipt and notice they gave you one penny too much money in change. Do you become faithful to the word of God, and go back in the store report the error and make it right, or is this amount to insignificance to report, in other words the decimal point is not significant. Perhaps many would agree this is no big deal, but what about an asset you purchased and now the decimal point is a $100 or $1000 or $10,000 dollar in your favor. Do you ignore it and *"draw-a-line-in-the-sand"* saying my faithfulness to the word of God is in the decimal point of everything less than "X-$ -amount" (I define the amount not God)…..?. Is this hitting home with you…….there are going to be test for you in the real world about this………what about being the best Christian you can be…….except during *"tax time"*…….?

What about the time you have to move and you are dating a girl you are probably going to get married, wow life would be so much easier if you…….."***moved-in together***"…….from a financial perspective, this makes logical sense. Is your faithfulness defined by a decimal point….. in real life situations? Are you making the observations of the scriptures, the correct interpretations of the scriptures with listening to the pastor (hopefully), yet when it comes to the **application** of the scripture and faithfulness in your own personal life are you making the application(s). Do you begin to see how God wants you to give him your faithfulness and how he wants you to grow in faithfulness?

It not just a "*nice*" biblical story it's an application to the biblical truths and should be written on the table of your heart. A code of faith you live by and honor the Lord thy God with respect and love for him. Grow in grace and in the faith of our Lord Jesus Christ. Do not let the level of your faith be defined by a decimal point in the world!

3.4   FAITHFULNESS WITH A FEW SHEEP

Is the level of your faithfulness to God's word directly portioned to a how big a task you are facing? When you are faithfully attending you church you may be given a simple task of doing something, like would you be a part of the greeting committee one Sunday out of the month. You try it and decide this is not for you, so you say no I don't want to serve in this capacity. Or do you take the opportunity to know God is in control and perhaps this is an area to start your spiritual growth. Remember how you can be put in charge of just a few sheep or a few things at first…….if you handle this well…….that is you can learn and grow and really engage in it, then you will be ready for bigger things, not to diminish the importance of the greeting committee, trust me it's critical and everyone in the church should take some role in greeting new people. The first assignment or task may not be your area of specialty, but when you are ask really try it for a while, this could lead to many other opportunities.

The lord reminds of how important it is for you to be faithful in the few things he allows you to handle in order to face major crisis or difficult days. Remember the story of David, this is what his father Jesse told "David" to do…….. 1s Samuel 17:17-22 And Jesse said unto David his son, Take now for thy brethren an ephah of this parched [corn], and these ten loaves, and run to the camp to thy brethren; 1Samuel 17:18 And carry these ten cheeses unto the captain of [their] thousand, and look how thy brethren fare, and take their pledge. 1Sameul 17:19 Now Saul, and they, and all the men of Israel, [were] in the valley of Elah, fighting with the Philistines. 1Samuel 17:20 ¶ And David rose up early in the morning, and left the sheep with a keeper, and took, and went, as Jesse had commanded him; and he came to the trench, as the host was going forth to the fight, and shouted for the battle. 1Sameul 17:21 For Israel and the Philistines had put the battle in array, army against army. 1Samuel 17:22 And David left his carriage in the hand of the keeper of the carriage, and ran into the army, and came and saluted his brethren. So you see David's oldest brother Eliab had no idea he had been given instruction(s) from his father Jesse and that David had made arrangements with another "*keeper*" to watch over the.......notice here "*few sheep*" or few items he had been entrusted with. Also notice how David had taken this task so seriously and engaged in lives of the "*few sheep*" aka **few things**, how it had prepared him for battle with the more serious difficulties or crisis we see him face now. Notice here the immortal words of Jesus Christ as he is saying in Matthew 25:21 His lord said unto him, Well done, [thou] good and faithful servant: thou hast been faithful over a **few things**, I will make thee ruler over many things: enter thou into the joy of thy lord.

God wants you to give your faithfulness when you are in charge of just a "few" sheep or a few items.......apply all your heart mind and soul in these few items there is a learning curve from God here........ learn all you can while in charge of just a few sheep, so God can prepare you for other service.

So see how the building blocks begin in your spiritual maturity....... as you walk daily with God. Let it begin slowly and deliberately watch as the story of David unfolds as he faces difficult crisis or giant problems here. We pick up again in 1st Samuel 17 And David left his carriage in the hand of the keeper of the carriage, and ran into the army, and came and saluted his brethren. Watch as one of the greatest bible stories unfolds here and notice how David defended his life for the few sheep that allowed him to be prepared to face far bigger and greater difficulties, notice how David is acting under the authority of his heavenly father and under the authority of his earthly dad...Jesse here:

1Samuel 17:23 And as he talked with them, behold, there came up the champion, the Philistine of Gath, Goliath by name, out of the armies of the Philistines, and spake according to the same words: and David heard [them]. 1 Samuel 17:24 And all the men of Israel, when they saw the man, fled from him, and were sore afraid. 1 Samuel 17:25 And the men of Israel said, Have ye seen this man that is come up? Surely to defy Israel is he come up: and it shall be, [that] the man who killeth him, the king will enrich him with great riches, and will give him his daughter, and make his father's house free in Israel. 1Samuel 17:26 And David spake to the men that stood by him, saying, What shall be done to the man that killeth this Philistine, and taketh away the reproach from Israel? For who [is] this uncircumcised Philistine, that he should defy the armies of the living God? 1Sameul 17:27 And the people answered him after this manner, saying, So shall it be done to the man that killeth him. 1Sameul 17:28 ¶ And Eliab his eldest brother heard when he spake unto the men; and Eliab's anger was kindled against David, and he said, Why camest thou down hither? And with whom hast thou left those few sheep in the wilderness? I know thy pride, and the naughtiness of thine heart; for thou art come down that thou mightest see the battle. 1Sameul 17:29 And David said, What have I now done? [Is there] not a cause? 1 Samuel 17:30 And he turned from him toward another, and spake after the same manner: and the people answered him again after the former manner. 1 Samuel 17:31 ¶ And when the words were heard which David spake, they rehearsed [them] before Saul: and he sent for him. 1Samuel 17:32 And David said to Saul, Let no man's heart fail because of him; thy servant will go and fight with this Philistine. 1Samuel 17:33 And Saul said to David, Thou art not able to go against this Philistine to fight with him: for thou [art but] a youth, and he a man of war from his youth. 1Samuel 17:34 And David said unto Saul, Thy servant kept his father's sheep, and there came a lion, and a bear, and took a lamb out of the flock: 1Samuel 17:35 And I went out after him, and smote him, and delivered [it] out of his mouth: and when he arose against me, I caught [him] by his beard, and smote him, and slew him. 1Sameul 17:36 Thy servant slew both the lion and the bear: and this uncircumcised Philistine shall be as one of them, seeing he hath defied the armies of the living God. 1Sameul 17:37 David said moreover, The LORD that delivered me out of the paw of the lion, and out of the paw of the bear, he will deliver me out of the hand of this Philistine. And Saul said unto David, Go, and the LORD be with thee. 1 Samuel 17:38 And Saul armed David with his armour, and he put an helmet of brass upon his head; also he armed him with a coat of mail. 1Sameul 17:39 And David girded his sword upon his armour, and he assayed to go; for he had not proved [it]. And David said unto Saul, I cannot go with these; for I have not proved [them]. And David put them off him. 1 Samuel 17:40 And he took his staff in his hand, and chose him five smooth stones out of the brook, and put them in a shepherd's bag which he had, even in a scrip; and his sling [was] in his hand: and he drew near to the Philistine. 1 Samuel 17:41 And the Philistine came on and drew near unto David; and the man that bare the shield [went] before him. 1Sameul 17:42 And when the Philistine looked about, and saw David, he disdained him: for he was [but] a youth, and ruddy, and of a fair countenance. 1Sameul 17:43 And the Philistine said unto David, [Am] I a dog, that thou comest to me with staves? And the Philistine cursed David by his gods. 1 Samuel 17:44 And the Philistine said to David, Come to me, and I will give thy flesh unto the fowls of the air, and to the beasts of the field.

1 Samuel 17:45 Then said David to the Philistine, Thou comest to me with a sword, and with a spear, and with a shield: but I come to thee in the name of the LORD of hosts, the God of the armies of Israel, whom thou hast defied. 1Sameul 17:46 This day will the LORD deliver thee into mine hand; and I will smite thee, and take thine head from thee; and I will give the carcases of the host of the Philistines this day unto the fowls of the air, and to the wild beasts of the earth; that all the earth may know that there is a God in Israel. 1Sameul 17:47 And all this assembly shall know that the LORD saveth not with sword and spear: for the battle [is] the LORD'S, and he will give you into our hands. 1Sameul 17:48 And it came to pass, when the Philistine arose, and came and drew nigh to meet David, that David hasted, and ran toward the army to meet the Philistine. 1 Samuel 17:49 And David put his hand in his bag, and took thence a stone, and slang [it], and smote the Philistine in his forehead, that the stone sunk into his forehead; and he fell upon his face to the earth. 1 Samuel 17:50 So David prevailed over the Philistine with a sling and with a stone, and smote the Philistine, and slew him; but [there was] no sword in the hand of David. 1 Samuel

17:51 Therefore David ran, and stood upon the Philistine, and took his sword, and drew it out of the sheath thereof, and slew him, and cut off his head therewith. And when the Philistines saw their champion was dead, they fled.

Do you see here how this ruddy youth, no one gave a chance to defeat a proven 7 & ½ foot warrior,*(height based on the dead sea scrolls)* that seem to be undefeatable, yet David with amazing **courage** and **faith** in God was able to slay the Giant......but notice even in their conversation David gave God glory........and David who was in charge of just a few sheep aka a few things was so engaged with all his heart mind and strength to defend those few sheep with his very life, and the lesson(s) it had taught him along the way......learning to slay the lion.......learning to slay the bear.......God had used him in a powerful and mighty way.......he had taken those **transferable skills** and slay yet another wild beast......Do you see how they told David you're not qualified, you're not trained for this, you're not old enough........but you see they had no knowledge of how God looks at a person and how God knows what a person is capable of doing when acting under the authority of God..........a lesson for the ages.

3.5   ENGAGE WITH ALL YOUR HEART

Do you see here how David was able to overcome the giant obstacle based on his being totally immersed and engaged in the few sheep his father Jesse had entrusted him, and taught him how to use the spear, sword, and sling shot, how many days had he practiced with what few items he had been given and perfected it to the point of hunting down the lion and bear and taking the lamb out of their mouth......he learned faithfulness of God through being in charge of a few things.......see how the building blocks begin? David did not say.....this is not my forte.... I am not talented at taking care of a few sheep.........I am not too good with this sling shot, or welding this sword.......no he practiced and worked at it until he became very proficient at it.....up to the point of defending his own life with the tools God had equipped him with . And notice David acted upon his Dad's authority......did exactly what his dad Jesse had instructed him to do...... and look how thy brethren fare, and take their pledge......this was his Dad's instructions....... David was acting under the authority given to him by his Dad. Notice he was taking the pledge of the men of war and seeing how they were *"sore afraid"* of the wild beast that was taunting them and they had under gone this for forty days. The King was not leading them into battle he was taller than all of them and should had been training and praying to combat this philistine, but instead he offered a handsome reward to have someone else eliminate his problem. Do you see how faithful David was to God, giving him Glory saying........ I will give the carcases of the host of the Philistines this day unto the fowls of the air, and to the wild beasts of the earth; that **all** the earth may know that there is a **God** in Israel. David had great faith in God!

We should follow this example and all have *"**great**"* faith in God.

1Corinthians 4:2 Moreover it is required in stewards, that a man be found **faithful.** God wants you to give him your faithfulness.

1Corintiians 4:17 For this cause have I sent unto you Timotheus, who is my beloved son, and **faithful** in the Lord, who shall bring you into remembrance of my ways which be in Christ, as I teach every where in every church. Teach faithfulness in Christ in all the churches.

1Corinthians 7:25 Now concerning virgins I have no commandment of the Lord: yet I give my judgment, as one that hath obtained mercy of the Lord to be **faithful**. God wants you to be faithful in sexual purity. Notice in the last verse I reference here this can be and should be applied to the males as well as females. Generally the terms is applied to females, but notice the term is not gender specific and should apply to males. We should reward and applaud our male youths for sexual purity and call them out accordingly that their lives be made pure in holding steadfast to God's commandment.

God wants you to give him your **faithfulness**.

4. GOD WANTS YOU TO GIVE QUITE TIME IN BIBLE STUDY

Where does it say this in scripture? Psalms 46:10 Be still, and know that I [am] God: I will be exalted among the heathen, I will be exalted in the earth. Be still have a quite time and know God is who he says he is and God can do what he says he can do, but you have a responsibility to be still and prayerfully read the scripture and grow in grace and knowledge of our Lord Jesus Christ. Here is where it says that in scripture. 1st peter 3:18 But grow in grace, and [in] the knowledge of our Lord and Saviour Jesus Christ. To him [be] glory both now and for ever. Amen.

So you see God wants you to give him quite time most notably early in the mornings like Abraham and David, but any time is good that you can actually give God to pray and study your bible. Notice here the scripture is saying grow in knowledge of our Lord and Savior, it did not say stop reading and stop growing after you get saved and perhaps baptized. This is just the beginning, so **start** the journey. Sometime our church puts on a "Judgment House" (walk through drama big production involves over 200 people) and we make the invitation to either have special prayer, rededicate your life to Christ, or pray to receive Jesus as your lord and personal savior. When someone prays to receive the lord and be saved, I suggest the starting point is with the proverbs because there are 31 days in the month and if they miss or skip a day they can pick back up on the calendar date. I also remind them this is just a starting point of reference and they can build on this, and should have a quite time with the Lord every day. This is essential for the young new Christian. Why not listen to what the scripture says: 1ˢᵗ Peter 2:2-3 As newborn babes, desire the sincere milk of the word, that ye may grow thereby: If so be ye have tasted that the Lord [is] gracious. Like a new born baby you should read the new testament 1ˢᵗ in my opinion moving onward through Jude, go back to the book of John and read it three times over. This establishes a firm foundation for you, please memorize John 14: 6. Jesus saith unto him, I am the way, the truth, and the life: no man cometh unto the Father, but unto me.

Write this verse on the table of your heart and understand it's all about a relationship with Jesus……..not about which church you belong to…..get that down pat and make that a part of who you are at the very core of your being.

4.1 WHERE DO I REALLY START WITH QUITE TIME

What if you have been a Christian for a long time and you need a new and fresh beginning, where do you start. I would say read 5 Psalms a day and if you get to a part of a verse that strikes you as something special, write this down, and the rest of the day meditate on the verse that jumped out at you. Ok what in the world does meditate on God's word mean, simple to think about it and rehearse it all day long in your mind? Go over it again and again, and pray to God that he will help **you** understand it as **you** meditate upon it. Help **you** understand that verse of scripture as it applies to **your** life, and what **you** need to learn. That is all mediate upon the word of God means it's very personal and applicable to **you**!

God wants you to give him quite time in bible study!

4.2 HOW OFTEN DO I HAVE QUITE TIME

Every day you have quite time with God, this has to be established by you, and not by anyone else because some people arrive at work 15 minutes early…….their time is so precious and every minute of the day is accounted for………so the small 15 minute window is all you have, take-it! I have a friend who once told me since he has (5) children the *"Tynnery-of-Urgency"* takes precedence over his entire life, I mean to say every single minute is accounted for in his day. So no matter what time he arrives at his parking space either late or early he mandates the (15) minutes of his day and he has proclaimed*" **what a difference***" this has made in his entire life on every level. See how this works. Daily scripture is what you need in your life and this goes back to the firstfruits process where you are giving the firstfruits of your day to God, and if you do this God will honor this. See how this all works together in a synergy of building blocks.

4.3   WHAT IF I DON'T WANT TO START IN PSALMS

Psalms is a good place to start but a wonderful place to start if you do not want to start in Psalms is Romans. Trust God on this one........and start here and read, meditate, and re-read Romans until you have many scripture verses highlighted. What I want to stress here is the value of this particular book it is filled with great virtue (morality) and it is wonderful. I have highlighted many scripture verses in Romans (good stuff) Let the word of God speak to your heart......Please Please Please start here I actually recommend it over Psalms......the best thing would be to read one Psalms and then one chapter of Romans.

4.4   WHAT IF I DON'T WANT TO START IN ROMANS

Your last chance is going to be start if nowhere else in the book of **John**......you know......Matthew, Mark Luke, & **John**. This is a great starting place too. The book of John is one of my favorite books in the bible, it is so awesome. So many truths in here, so many black and white issues it's either going for....or.....against god, but one of the main points is the badge of a Christian.......and that being "Love". Compassion for one another, and letting your light so shine that others may see the love and compassion you have for others. I have heard it said this way for people who don't go to church and people who have no intentions of ever going to church, then in some cases "**You**" are the closest thing to Jesus they will ever see!

Think about it......they need to see the salt and light in you....... please pass the salt........be that inner light and make them see something different in you....what can they see......if you will let God change you from the inside out and not curse, not act foolishly, be sober, and try your best to follow God's laws and commandments at some point even if they don't want to see it, they will begin to see it, and say there is something special about him/her……and that is what is meant when we say please pass the salt, always making your own light visible to others…….teaching others the flavor of your Christianity especially by your own actions……… Let other see a change in you……..when and if they ask…………tell them it's the synergy affect that happens, once you start teaching others about who Jesus…..was….is…..and is to come. You can lead by example if you will let the Lord Jesus change you from within, allow God to work in your life. Read the book of **John** three times.

4.5 WHAT IF I DON'T START IN PSALMS, ROMANS, OR JOHN, THEN WHAT?

Start in Genesis this is from the beginning and you have to start here last stop, start at the beginning and move onward. Genesis should be done if possible with video's and bible study groups because sometimes you can get so much more out of these verses if you have some extra study help, even though you could say that about any book of the bible, but this is especially true with Genesis. This is a top down approach, and a good one, but it really helps if you go all the way through to the end of the bible as quickly as possible if you start this way……it gives you an overall baseline and then you can come back and focus on certain books one at a time, drill down even deeper……The word of God is a living breathing truth formula for…….your life!

4.6 GOD WANTS ME TO GIVE MEDIATATION ON HIS WORD

Here is what you do if you don't like any of the choices I have suggested here, find out what your preacher is preaching on each week and read the chapter before and chapter after…….then read the chapter he is going to be preaching on Sunday morning….This will greatly get you plugged-in to his sermons and you can follow easily along with his preaching. This is a very good way to go, and often times now churches have the pastor's sermons posted online, so even if you miss you can go back and get "plugged-in". Start somewhere and just engage in the word. If you're still lost and don't have any idea where to begin after all the suggestions, then start in a place you choose, but try and make a logical choice like you start in the Old testament or the New testament , or choose a book of poetry, history, prophetical, or one of my favorite's the book of **John**. Luke is a good starting place too, along with Matthew, or Mark. Point being.......make a choice and start. I should mention here you can get a bible dictionary and when you come to a word that is "*baffling*"........ pull out the bible dictionary and consult it, this adds great insight into the passage of scripture you're reading. You can also have a bible commentary handy, so this is what to do, read a passage of scripture one time through, get an idea of who the characters are what the culture is like, what events are transpiring, who the main character(s) are, and what is happening in the passage. I would read it first in a modern plain English version, so you know "**what**" is going on. Then after you read the story through one time now go back and start drilling down in the story, what is happening, with the "children of Israel" **what** is God teaching them, **why** is this important that God teaches them this......? Then see if you can go back a third time, but this time before you read it, ask God to help **revel to you the personal message you need** to receive of this particular passage of scripture. Read the commentaries, read the bible dictionary and any other reference materials you have gathered on this particular passage of scripture. When you do this it makes the word come alive and be so much more vivid in your own life instead of just pulling one page of scripture out reading it and saying I read my scripture for the day.

There is a lost art here called meditation, and most Christians think this is some kind of trance where you sit cross-legged and saying "umnmmmmmm".......or something. God desires that you think about his word and spend hour's thinking about his word(s) because God's words are good for you mind, body, & soul. I know I have mentioned this already and keep harping on it, but it is so important to your well being. God really does want you to mediate on his word......how do I know this......scripture says so.....really where: Psalms 1:2 But his delight [is] in the law of the LORD; and in his law doth he **meditate** day and night. Psalms 63:6-7 When I remember thee upon my bed,

[and] **meditate** on thee in the [night] watches. Because thou hast been my help, therefore in the shadow of thy wings will I rejoice.

God wants you to give **mediate** on his word!

5. GOD WANTS YOU TO GIVE HIM SACRIFICES

This cannot be right. Sacrifice, I mean isn't that some of the "*old school*" or you know "old testament" stuff…..the modern church does not condone a person giving sacrifices right…? Well this has changed along with our culture, what God wants you to get here……..is that sacrifice in our culture is often our precious commodity involving our "*Time*". In the old days…….there was prayer, and a lot of time to think about God as they prepared the animal sacrifice. Our personal time we could spend on our favorite hobby; napping, eating, playing, or just the……..."me" time……you have to actually give up some of this precious time, and sacrifice it to God. God wants you to be still and know above all else he alone is God and he created you, loves you, and knows you, better than you know yourself, but he wants a very personal relationship with you and him. Therefore, you have to give up some of your precocious time and "*share-it*" with your one true God. A chance to give back that which is so freely given and taken without words of justification, just a moment of sharing the intimacy of the relationship with God. With clean hands and a pure heart you come to humble yourself before the Almighty God, asking God to purge any iniquities or forwardness from you. This will allow you to have peace on a level that surpasses any understanding. To have the peace of God in your heart is to keep your mind stayed on thee as God's word tells us in Isaiah 26:3 He will keep him in perfect peace whose mind is stayed on thee.

God wants you to give a sacrifice of time to him.......to share intimacy with him!

5.1   HOW DO I KNOW WHAT MY TALENTS ARE…?

Ask yourself these self-examining question(s):
Prayerfully ask God:

- What am I good at?

- What do I enjoy doing?

- Has the Holy Spirit given me peace about what God has called me to do?

- Do I encourage others to help build the body of Christ?

Once you do an examination and pray over this........God will help reveal this to you.

Here is the hard part........Wait on God to reveal this to you by **circumstances**, or **in his word**, or he just puts the knowledge in your heart where you **know that you know**.

- Psalms 130:5-6 I wait for the lord, my soul doth wait, and in his word do I hope. My soul waiteth for the Lord more than they that watch for the morning: I say , more than they the watch for the morning.

- Psalms 27:14 Wait on the Lord: Be of good courage, and he shall strengthen thine heart.

- Psalms 40:1 I waited patiently for the Lord; and he inclined unto me, and heard my cry.

- Psalms 62:5 My soul, wait thou only upon God; for my expectation is from him.

Another way to help assist in this answer is simply doing the following: read these (5) passages and understand there common interest is staying in church being a part of the fellowship of God. Being a part of God's people trying your very best to live according to God's statues and commandments. Really trying, meaning if you are living outside the will of God you get down on your knees repent and turn 180 degrees from that direction(s), no fooling yourself. True repentance is making change. James 5:16 "Therefore, confess your sins to one another, and pray for one another so that you may be healed. The effective prayer of a **righteous man** can accomplish much. "So you see you are to be in church to pray and confess you sins one to another, not watch church on TV be there in person to consult and confess your sins one to another and lift up each other in prayer because as it is written the prayer of a righteous man availed much, well who is a righteousness man…..the man that does not forsake the assembly. Let's look at another reason why you should be in church Thessalonians 5:11 wherefore comfort yourselves together, and edify one another, even as also ye do. What this means is to comfort and lift up one another helping each other out any way you can, example it may be as simple as a one day a week car pool or allowing a neighbor to borrow a chain saw instead of having to rent one, and maybe they will take you out to dinner for the kind deed. Then read this 1st Peter 4:10 As every man hath received the gift, even so minister the same one to another, as good stewards of the manifold grace of God. In other words, once you have discovered your gift you should be in the world sharing your "*gift-of-grace*" with others, and even at individual homes if necessary. Notice the bible is absolute here every man, not just a few or some men…….that is all men! AMEN! Come on now get on board with me here……..AMEN! Lastly just so you know…….Hebrews 10:25 Not forsaking the assembling of ourselves together, as the manner of some is; but exhorting one another and so much the more, as ye see the day approaching. What this is saying is do not error brethren……. here it is…….crystal clear you are to meet **in person** in the assembly to be an encouragement to one another. Can God make it any clearer for you than this? If others see you consistently, it is an encouragement that you are dedicated to worship the Lord. It helps all the assembly, and I have found unbelievable friendships and blessing and help along the way. God's knows in his infinite wisdom you need the fellowship of the brethren. I am a shy and a bashful person who is very introverted (like to keep to myself) but if you will allow God to work on you from the inside out…..you will be amazed at what God can do with your own individual shyness and bashfulness……what…..he can actually change you…..no way…..yes way….baby steps but he can do it. But you have to do your part……what is my part on the shyness……..pray and believe and ask God to help you take the 1st step within your own church….. maybe it's just going out to dinner after Sunday Service……but it helps eating with a small group of people from your own church it works……. even if you are all eating at a Pizza place it develops relationships…… God is an incredible God. Sometimes talking to the brethren you can discover a need or talent in an area you have not thought of……?

Sometimes for health purposes you cannot actually attend the assembly…….this is understandable, but once you are healthy enough to attend go down to the alter and thank the good Lord for the "health" to attend his assembly, God is the great Physician and he can cure **any** illness, but there is an active part you should partake of …… remember when Jesus healed 10 lepers, only *"one-out-of-ten"* came back and thanked Jesus……Never forget this………the Lord giveth, and the Lord taketh away!

God wants you to give your **talents** to serve him, but first discover your talents!

5.2   GIVING GOD YOUR AVAILABILITY

Let me start here with saying once you have identified you spiritual gifts and once you are at peace with you talents then you should…….of your own free will and accord…serve god because you are grateful for the blessing he has bestowed upon you. It is an honor and privilege to serve God and what an honor and privilege to have the health to worship and sing praises to your God.

My own personal talents……..I was raised in a church and I went to Sunday school from the time I was little (in my mother's womb) till I was in college. I majored in geology, worked in accounting most of my adult life (explain that one) then I went to several different denominations/ churches. I had no idea what my spiritual gifts were or that I even had any….let me stress this one again…..**any**……..spiritual gifts. I thought I can't sing, I can't preach, I have no talents. Well I remember standing in the sanctuary at Morning Side Baptist Church praying to God when I was searching for a church home in Tallahassee Florida…….. at an age of 44 years old…..praying to God…..help me find a church and for once in my life God **I** will not choose the church, you my Lord and Savior......choose the church home for me.......God will you help reveal to me the church where I am to serve you........a great peace came over me that very moment and the most incredible feeling that Dale for once a breakthrough in your own personal life.....this is the church I would have you serve in..........I had such perfect peace and felt like I was home. I realize the church was about 25 minutes from my house and I have come to realize what a beautiful time this has allowed for my wife and I.......in quality time to and from church......sometimes I enjoy a motorcycle ride in the back roads to and from church...... but I have found peace there. So what talents did I have.......were they lockup inside me.......and I did not know what they were. The Sunday School director had been praying and seeking God for a new Sunday school teacher.....they ask me and my wife Michele if we would teach College and Career........I was shocked, I thought they had the wrong couple perhaps they had made a mistake, but after freaking out a little, ok a lot, and then going to God in prayer about it........Michele and I became the feeble College and Career Sunday School teachers. We even went on a youth trip to Panama City Florida and had some good times with the youth........this was not my talent though.......I was better off teaching adults.....and eventually (a year later) God switched the college and career from me to another talented guy, and I taught adults from age 40-70.....let me say this now if you had ask me to teach a class of adults I would have said I am not qualified or trained to do so......but God has provided and equipped me to do so in a "co-teacher" environment. I have learned more along the way than I ever thought possible, and have just been *"blow-away"* at how God has worked in the shy bashful introverted person of who I am.......unbelievable.....I want to mention this.....if they had ask me to teach adults 40 & over I would have jumped ship and headed for the boarder........I get and understand a little bit about Jonah now.

I have been a scene director in our walk through drama, I have been a counselor, I have served in the counting committee(accounting people who count the money & balance the books), I have been serving as a usher when needed, I have served on the finance committee, I have served on the personnel committee, and I am amazed at how God has shown me what I **can do**........when I was convinced I had no.... **no talents**......but see how getting involved in your local church and

allowing God to work in your life can reveal opportunities to you.......
you never thought were possible.

God wants you to give you **availability** to him, so he can reveal to
you how he can use your talents to serve him.

5.3   GIANTS TO OVERCOME

So what about using your talents to serve God? 1st Samuel 16:17 but the
Lord said unto Samuel, look not on his countenance or on the height of
his stature; because I have refused him: for the Lord seeth not as man
seeth; for man looketh on the outward appearance, but the Lord looketh
on the heart. God sees you differently. When David was anointed he
was not a typical looking King. God saw through to his heart and God
knew his heart.......and God was pleased to train him, equipment him,
and have his spirit upon him. You see you might not even realize it,
but God has been training you all your life for his calling. Watch and
see.......let's look at a conversation David had with his eldest brother
Eliab. 1s Samuel 17:28 and Eliab his eldest brother heard when he spake
unto the men; and Elab's anger was kindled against David, and he
said, Why camest tho done hither? And with whom has tho left those
few sheep in the wilderness I know they pride, and the naughtiness of
thin heart; for tho are come done that thou mightest see the battle.
And David said, What have I now done? Is there not a cause. You see
David's oldest brother had no idea what God was planning and what
miracle was about to transpire and instead of lifting-up or encouraging
his brother, he was tearing him down. Don't tell me.........no such
thing as spiritual warfare does not exist. It really does exist and never
forget Ephesians 6:12 For we wrestle not against flesh and blood, but
against principalities, against powers, against rulers of the darkness in
high places. Not only will you face opposition but you will face doubt
and fears as you try and use your talents to serve God. You see Eliab was
in King Saul's army away from home he did not have any knowledge
of this conversation between David and his Dad Jesse. 1st Samuel 17:
17-18 And Jesse said unto David his son, Take now for thy brethren and
ephah of this parched corn, and these ten loaves, and run to the camp
to thy brethren; and carry these ten cheeses unto the captain of their
thousand, and look how they brethren fare, and take their pledge. So
David was acting under the authority of his God, by being submissive

to his Dad's instructions, but his eldest brother had no idea why or what he was doing there. So David was to deliver food and take the pledge of his brethren and report back to Jesse his dad. Notice the **secret** Eliab revealed to us in his lambasting words.........few sheep........David had been in charge of a "**few-sheep**" not a lot of sheep just a **few sheep**. What's the difference....? He had been trained since he was a young lad to care for the sheep even risking his life for the live stock of the sheep, and he did this with all his heart and a strong and fervent belief in God above. In verse 20 notice the care David took for the few sheep. 1st Samuel 17:20 And David rose early in the morning, and left the sheep with a keeper, and took and went as Jesse had commanded him; and he came to the trench as the host was going forth to the fight, and shouted for the battle. Notice here he was not in charge of an entire massive flock just a **few sheep** why.......This was exactly what God needed to stress to David the importance of his mission and train him to defend the livestock with his life, God had him exactly where he needed him for his training. Notice how God had prepared David to combat wild beast, a lion and a bear, where David had learned to use a sling, a stone, and a sword defeated the wild beast even rescuing the lamb from the wild beast's mouth. See how God was preparing him for a bigger picture in Israel, but by being faithful and serving with **all his heart** right where God had planted him he was honoring God. And God honor David being submissive to the authority of God, and the authority of his earthly dad Jesse. Notice, David did not complain, or mummer, or quit, or give-up, David "**bloomed**" right where God had planted him...... and David put his heart / mind / actions in everything he did.

Notice David and Jesse did not have a conversation where David said I'm not all that good with this sling, I am getting a blister practicing throwing this sword, or my arm hurts practicing with this sling........... No...David had determination, and trusted in God!

God wants you to **overcome** Giant obstacle(s) in your life, by blooming where you are planted!

1st Samuel 17:32 And David said to Saul, Let no man's heart fail because of him; they servant will go and fight this Philistine. Notice the **courage** it took to say this to the King of Israel at that day and time..... the King who could with an "*unquestionable*"...."*word/order*" have you killed at will.......just because he was in the mood. But notice how the

King himself looked upon the outward appearance of the Giant 7.1/2 feet Philistine (the average height of most men in this day and time was around 5'5") and then King Saul looked at the small little Israelite and said this.........1ˢᵗ Samuel 17:33 And Saul said to David, tho are not able to go against this Philistine to fight with him for thou art but a youth, , and he a man of war from his youth. Notice more spiritual warfare, King Saul had no idea what God's plans were. King Saul was a foot or so taller than most men in the land and he should have been the one as the leader to train and fight the Philistine for his people.......leading by example, ah but King Saul hid behind the lack of courage, and tried to weasel around this situation very politically speaking.......offering a generous reward for the Israelite that would fight the Philistine Giant. Notice here in Chapter 17:25 And the men of Israel said, have ye seen this man that is come up? Surely to defy Israel is he come up: and it shall be, that the man who killeth him, the king will enrich him with great riches, and will give him his daughter, and make his father's house (tax) free in Israel. It would appear Saul is probably after about 40 days of having this Giant insult and defy the army of Israel he started out with a reward of Riches, then upped it to his daughter in marriage (instant nobility), then upped it finally to having the man's family be tax exempt. But nowhere is it mentioned here about King Saul's height or goodliness here........Notice in Chapter 9 verse 2 "And he had a son, whose name was Saul, a choice young man, and goodly; and there was not among the children of Israel a **goodlier** person than he from his shoulders and upward he was **higher than any of the people**. So we should mention he was a good person, and he was head and shoulders taller than anyone in Israel. He was the King and leader and he should have led by example, but just like you and me he was looking out for number one, instead of God's interest, and God's plans. Notice how the conversation transpires with David and how doubtful and how King Saul wanted a front line seat.....for what King Saul assuredly thought would be a "*slaughter-of-the-youth*". Notice and focus on the conversation here: 1ˢᵗ Samuel 17:34-40. And David said unto Saul, Thy servant kept his father's sheep, and there came a lion, and a bear, and took a lamb out of the flock: And I went out after him, and smote him, and delivered [it] out of his mouth: and when he arose against me, I caught [him] by his beard, and smote him, and slew him. Thy servant slew both the lion and the bear: and this uncircumcised Philistine shall be as one of them, seeing he hath defied the armies of the living God. David said moreover, The LORD that delivered me out of the paw of the lion, and out of the paw of the bear, he {GOD} will deliver me out of the hand of this Philistine. And Saul said unto David, **Go**, and the LORD be with thee. And Saul armed David with his armour, and he put an helmet of brass upon his head; also he armed him with a coat of mail. And David girded his sword upon his armour, and he assayed to go; for he had not proved [it]. And David said unto Saul, I cannot go with these; for I have not proved [them]. And David put them off him. And he took his staff in his hand, and chose him five smooth stones out of the brook, and put them in a shepherd's bag which he had, even in a scrip; and his sling [was] in his hand: and he drew near to the Philistine. David gives his credentials and they are good ones how many Israelites had actually fought a bear and lion in "*hand-to-hand-combat*" to get food out of the wild beast mouth......probably not many if any. You can see King Saul's goodliness he offers the best chain mail armor and the best weapons.......but when he sees the youth going forth like he came to him are King Saul's thoughts of let's watch the slaughter, do I up the reward with riches or what if this guy fails........look at him a sling shot and a club...this can't be good. What is the one possibility that you and I forget..........Chapter 16 Verse 13 the critical part of what you and I need to remember forever in our mind and conscious......13 Then Samuel took the horn of oil, and anointed him in the midst of his brethren; and the **spirit of the Lord came upon David from that day forward**. So Samuel rose up, and went to Ramah. Notice here the spirit of the Lord is upon David............that makes all the difference in the world. Pick up again in the Chapter 17 and notice how David faced the giant.....Listen to the conversation and how David gives God glory even in his conversation: And the Philistine came on and drew near unto David; and the man that bare the shield [went] before him. And when the Philistine looked about, and saw David, he disdained him: for he was [but] a youth, and ruddy, and of a fair countenance. And the Philistine said unto David, [Am] I a dog, that thou comest to me with staves? And the Philistine cursed David by his gods. And the Philistine said to David, Come to me, and I will give thy flesh unto the fowls of the air, and to the beasts of the field. Then said David to the

Philistine, Thou comest to me with a sword, and with a spear, and with a shield: but I come to thee in the name of the LORD of hosts, the God of the armies of Israel, whom thou hast defied. This day will the LORD deliver thee into mine hand; and I will smite thee, and take thine head from thee; and I will give the carcases of the host of the Philistines this day unto the fowls of the air, and to the wild beasts of the earth; that all the earth may know that there is a God in Israel. And all this assembly shall know that the LORD saveth not with sword and spear: for the battle [is] the LORD'S, and he will give you into our hands. And it came to pass, when the Philistine arose, and came and drew nigh to meet David, that David hasted, and ran toward the army to meet the Philistine. And David put his hand in his bag, and took thence a stone, and slang [it], and smote the Philistine in his forehead, that the stone sunk into his forehead; and he fell upon his face to the earth. So David prevailed over the Philistine with a sling and with a stone, and smote the Philistine, and slew him; but [there was] no sword in the hand of David. Therefore David ran, and stood upon the Philistine, and took his sword, and drew it out of the sheath thereof, and slew him, and cut off his head therewith. And when the Philistines saw their champion was dead, they fled. Awesome story........awesome story.........worth repeating again.........but what does this have to do with you?

You see when you begin to serve God with your talents, you're going to be met with opposition, persecution, and you will be under spiritual attack, you can't do that.... you're not qualified...you're not properly trained for that...you're not equipped for such a task. Sound familiar, ever heard this resonate in your own mind....or someone say this to you....?

Any time you come under attack you read this story again and again. God has prepared you for service and he had equipped you with all that you need to start. God had and will bring you along with transferable skills to completely serve him. Notice here David was not "properly-trained as a skilful warrior" in the sight of King Saul and others, but nevertheless David saw the transferrable skills and knew...

....I can face a wild beast such as this uncircumcised Philistine. It was just a bear or lion that had to be stunned in the head and then run through with a spear or sword, he knew the bear and lion had prepared him and running at the bear or the lion confused the wild beast and kept them from executing an offensive attack plan.......it put them on the defensive mode to react, and think how confused the Giant Goliath must have been when this small boy with a sling shot and a stick came running at him........Goliath was probably thinking what on earth is this kid doing he's no warrior he is going to run into me bounce off of me flat on his back or something, when all of a sudden the rock hit him and "**Sunk into**" his skull too late! Maybe this was the way David had attacked the lion and the bear......by running straight towards them stepping into the throw with maximum force of the sling shot. Think about this David.......had time to practice with his slingshot while being the Sheppard of just a **few sheep**. David had time to reflect on the lion attack, and the bear attack. Just imagine how David felt when he held the head of the Giant and shook it at the Philistine Army............ what a Victory of God......and notice how David gave glory to God.

Back to you, when you start to serve God with your talents don't quit at the 1st obstacle or 1st insurmountable problem draw on your past experiences and see if you can work out the problem analytically speaking.......based on your past experiences. Allow God to work in your life.

David's son was given more than any man on earth, over 700 wives and 300 something concubines, over 25 tons of gold per year etc........ hear the words of the one God granted more wisdom to… than to any other man: Ecclesiastes 12:13 Let us hear the conclusion of the whole matter: Fear God, and keep his commandments: for this [is] the whole [**duty**] of man. Your Duty is to Serve the most High God and keep his commandments; this is something you have to work on every day, and notice this is in the present tense not the past tense or future tense it is in the very moment of your life as you live day by day.

God wants you to give freely of your talents to serve him!

6. GOD WANTS YOU TO GIVE INVESTMENTS

6.1   INVESTMENTS IN RELATIONSHIPS

Toughest chapter in the book, and often in life.

Who pushes your **buttons** the most "FAMILY" and where do the most dysfunctional relationships exists within the.......interim family. There is a good reason God wants you to fix things in your house 1ˢᵗ before you can serve the most high God.

Look at the descriptions for a Pastor or Preacher, they use the old and ancient term Bishop here but notice what it says about his own home. 1 Timothy 3:2 A bishop then must be blameless, the husband of one wife, vigilant, sober, of good behaviour, given to hospitality, apt to teach Not given to wine, no striker, not greedy of filthy lucre; but patient, not a brawler, not covetous; One that ruleth well his own house, having his children in subjection with all gravity; (For if a man know not how to rule his own house, how shall he take care of the church of God?) Not a novice, lest being lifted up with pride he fall into the condemnation of the devil. Moreover he must have a good report of them which are without; lest he fall into reproach and the snare of the devil.

The one point lots of people fail to see here is this............having the authority and knowledge to "rule his own house well". In other words their relationship within are not in constant turmoil because the investments in the relationships are working toward fixing one another's "needs" and "goals", and helping one another in love, not spite, not in expectations of returned favors, just out of love expecting "**nothing**" in return, **nothing.** Believe it or not everyone has a role to play, and when you allow the person to fulfill the role in accordance to God's word, and dare I say actually help them fulfill their role, harmony abounds. Example it is the child's role to obey their parents and be submissive to their authority, not to make decisions. When both parents embrace this concept and help the child in that role, make sure the child cleans their room........this helps train the child how to properly clean their room, and follow up with why.......the child is in this particular role......what it is teaching them in life, and why, then the parents are properly rewarding them for good behavior stressing the points of authority where they need to be ....then the role of the child is more meaningful. This applies to each role Man, Wife, Child. Problems occur where the lines get crossed, blurry or gray. Even with great communication this can occur, so what happens when this occurs, each family member needs to extend.......loving (brotherly / sisterly) kindness of one another, and move onward. Try and fix a problem if possible to where it is never a problem again in your marriage / life. Example: Tuesday night is vacuum night, who does it......I did it last week she did it the week before ....one of you take the role of Tuesday night vacuum person, so this a non-issue, if possible every week the "guy" takes Tuesday nights and vacuums.........while he is doing this she cleans the bathrooms ....or reverse this every six months or whatever works for your family. But try to avoid discussion on who is doing what particular role when, where, why, and how. Define the roles and adhere to them......works differently for each family.

6.2   MY FAMILY IS TOO COMPLEX

Well there....... there now.......that's some mighty fine talking and sounds great, but you don't understand what all.......I and my family have been through, this would take a team of the best phsychologists in the country **years** to work out the problems this can't be fixed over night. You are correct here, this is a complex situation and in my opinion only "God" can work this out, not a team of the best phsychologists in the world (and all the phsychologists just screamed out loud) . So let me help you here.......most mental problems break down into....... immorality, bitterness, (deep hurt), or greed. When you trace it back to the core essential problem.......it fits into one of this three categories or some complex interweaving of them, (and all the phsychologists world-wide just screamed out loud again) If you come to your brother or sister and ask for a [one-on-one-meeting] with the person you have a conflict with and say to them......I have done wrong because of my greed, immorality, or bitterness, will you pray with me, when they hear you pray and know "*beyond a shadow of a doubt*" you are in sincerity of regret, and want to amend the relationship then ask them if they will work with you.......to work on the wrong "**you have done**" then progress can be made, because when two work together to resolve a relationship problem and prayer is involved you allow the holy spirit of God to intercede and miracles do happen. Pride has to be put asunder, easily said.........difficulty doing.

If you can **humble**.......yourself.......Your life can be changed forever "*for-the-better*"! I have seen this first hand and the powerful impact it takes on an otherwise broken and irrecoverable relationship. It requires swallowing **all** your pride and some **real time prayer** with the Lord asking for the words to say and asking if he will touch the heart of the person you need to work with. Never allow pride to resurface, the only way to do this is with "daily" prayer, sometime hourly prayer!

6.3   THE FAMILY WANTS TO JUST PICK UP WHERE WE LEFT OFF

What happens when you have gone through several years of drama and this one family member wants to just pick up where we last left our relationship as broken as it was and just move forward like nothing has happened. Yet you still have all this built up animosity towards them for all the drama over the past number of years. Here is a more difficult situation and this has no easy......one slate wipe cleaning or fix. Write down a list of the issues you want to go over and write down a list of the best case scenarios and worst case scenarios, then try to work on the best case scenarios and above all else ask yourself the question............ how much forgiveness should I actually do....really..................is that number beyond 490 times. Listen to Luke 6:41-42 And why beholdest thou the mote that is in thy brother's eye, but perceivest not the beam that is in thine own eye? Either how canst thou say to thy brother, Brother, let me pull out the mote that is in thine eye, when thou thyself beholdest not the beam that is in thine own eye? Thou hypocrite, cast out first the beam out of thine own eye, and then shalt thou see clearly to pull out the mote that is in thy brother's eye. Search long and hard within your own heart 1st and ask the recipient if they would consider working with you to resolve some differences and be patience. You know the ancient word for this modern word is "Longsuffering".......we now use patience, but I think the ancient term is more applicable and descriptive. Most of the time if you are organized write down a "**few**" things on the list not hundred(s) and ask the recipient to work with you......step by step you can achieve your goals. Never give up; God **never** gave up on you!!!

This will take some time, this will take some longsuffering, this will take your willingness to work through the problem(s).......Make a small list and if the person comes to you with a list, don't make fun of their list, don't dismiss their list, it is important to them so work through it and try to discover why & what you're doing and they are doing to overcome. You both have to come to the same conclusion......we both want deliverance/freedom from the current haunting issue(s). Unless you both come to this conclusion, it will be very difficult to work through the problem. Start conversations with what can I do to help you......and when a suggestion is out there you don't like ask for some time to think about it......Example what can I do to help you with this issue.......Stop asking me when the task will be finished........wow say you hated that response.........follow up with........ this particular task has a time limit......and I can't complete the next phase until your phase is completed......what is the appropriate time to follow up........ maybe not daily but check with you on "Fridays" and see where you are in the progress.....do you need me to do anything that is holding up the show......?

Still there is no easy response to these difficult task you **both** have to **work** together....Keep reminding each other we are working together on this.....we will work through the problem. Have you prayed together about it today...??? Have you prayed for the other person, has the other person prayed for you......do you believe in the prayers you prayed.........start believing.........keep the optimistic attitude. I want to remind you here of God's word notice it says in Philippians 2:14 Do all things without murmurings and disputings: Notice it says all things not just some things........make yourself become an optimistic person, always find something good to say no matter how bad the situation gets find something good to say. People do not like being around other people who are constantly complaining and negative. Make this character trait a part of who you are.......try this for 21 days in a row.....give it a go....try and only speak when you have something good to say........(raising children is often time the exception on this one) but to other adults and if possible try your best to be optimistic as possible to your children. God wants you to give an optimistic attitude by doing all things without murmuring or complaining.

7. GOD WANTS YOU TO GIVE THE GOSPEL TO THE LOST

There is a very specific reason I listed this one last and that is because I feel like you need to be aware of and fully "trained" before you go out and try to win souls for the lord. Some men have said you cannot do anything to screw this up.......just do it. I differ slightly in saying there is a time and place.......and learning to find that moment and being sensitive to the "*moment that presents itself*" is very critical to a person's ability to receive the message? Why.....it takes the average person 7.2 times.......of hearing the message of Christ before they will accept the truth of it. Why.....I am not sure, but you do not have any idea if that person is on their 1st time 3rd time, above average, below average, and intelligence cannot be a measure here, all are different, so some brilliant doctors may actually need more that 7.2 times......that is just an average, as other may need more that 7.2 times of hearing. Let me stress this "Faith comes by hearing, and hearing by the word of God. Romans 10:17 so let's ask this a different way.......do you want to increase your faith......? If the answer is yes.......keep reading, but reading with quality or "quality reading" is worth more than just reading in the blind "*sorta-speak*". I mean if you pick up the bible point blank open it at random and start reading, sometimes you find yourself saying who or what is going on here, as opposed to more of a **structured approach**.

Back on point, sharing the faith should be done in a **loving kind way**. I have seen this shared in a very abrasive and aggressive way all to no avail. I have seen it shared in a loving and kind way and some of the message took root. I am not saying there is a right and wrong way to do this, I am saying there…should be some thought in the process. Before you go to the man about God……..1ˢᵗ go to God about the man.

I have been on both sides of this equation and I am telling you praying to God about the man you're going to 1ˢᵗ makes…….a huge difference. I don't know how prayer works, it just works and that's all I know.

7.1   SHARING GPT

Sharing how on earth do I share? 1ˢᵗ of all there are many many many ways but a very good tool to have in your tool box is what I call the **GPT** and that needs to be in your tool box and practiced often. It's very simple and very good. Here is how it goes: (good person test) **GPT**

Do you think you are a good person and going to heaven…?

1.   Have you ever in your entire life told a lie?
2.   Have you ever in your entire life stolen anything?
3.   Have you ever in your entire life used the Lord's name in vain?
4.   Have you ever in your entire life hated anyone?

Then by your own admission you are a lying thieving blasphemous, murder at heart and if a "Holy God" judged you for this heaven…….
would not be your destination, so now that you know you're not going to heaven by **God's law** would you like to change that and invite Jesus into your heart as your lord and personal savior. Pray with me.

God wants you to share, use this tool when appropriate!

7.2   SHARING TRACTS

Some people have trouble using the GPT test for whatever reason, so another good method to share is to find a really good tract and let me stress the key is **good tract** and you just give them out and if you have time explain it page by page to a close friend. I recommend the "**chick publications**" tracts…….they are great art work, and easy to read, and straight forward to follow. It really helps here if you can make the presentation and show them the track step by step. And no, "*chick* *publications*" did not ask me to mention their name here.......this just happens to be a tract I am familiar with, and really like, my dad used to share them and explain them to me step by step......when I was a little boy.

7.3   SHARING PERSONAL TESTIMONY

I want to mention the best witness tool.......for close friends and relatives.......is your own personal testimony, and one of the best ways to do this is in a "*one-on-one*" luncheon or when you are isolated and have their full attention. Just explain what God has done for you how you were saved........if tears come down your check during the testimony believe me.......that make(s) your testimony greater.

Let the other person see your passion and heartfelt emotion as you tell.......your greatest story ever told.........and they know you have been changed forever. Let them see the joy and light in your life. From that day forward, after you share with them follow up frequently and ask them if you can pray for them over the phone from time to time when you see them.

During Thanksgiving go around the table with the family and share testimonies what God is currently doing in your life. Often time families say what they are thankful for, and lots of jokes and comments are made, but why not share your testimony of what God is currently doing in your life present day. That carries a weight and has impact. If you say not much is going on everything is fine, let me ask you this question are you spiritually where you need to be? Be real with your-self are you growing in the grace and in knowledge of Christ Jesus our Lord and savior? If you are green you grow if you're not you rot......some have said.............I say did you read 1ˢᵗ Peter 3:18 But grow in grace, and [in] the knowledge of our Lord and Saviour Jesus Christ. To him [be] glory both now and for ever. Amen.

The reason I ask if you know everything the bible has to teach you about Jesus then you are indeed special and probably not in the realm of earth. I learn things every day the more I study his word the more he reveals to me. Are you growing in knowledge have you read your bible today.......accountability check? If you are growing in grace you always have a word to say about God's goodness and God's glory in your own life, maybe things are good and you are just praising God for his goodness and mercy.

God wants you to share, use this tool when appropriate!

7.4　SHARING VIA YOUR OWN CHRUCH MINISTRIES

Another method besides the good person test and personal testimony is being a part of the ministry of children like a program at our church entitled "good news club" or if children are not your thing, then part of a ministry at your church perhaps "prison ministry" the people often forgotten. Get plugged into your own church ministries. You will be surprised at how God can, and will work in and through you…..if you will only let him.

Another method to sharing the gospel to the lost is always be sensitive to the conversations you have with people you just meet and looking for a moment to find out who they are and what they represent. You can tell a lot by a conversation with a person especially how worldly they are sometimes count the cruse words they use in a sentence……. that speaks volumes about who and where they are in life

Once you establish a bond with them…..**think……loving kind way**……this should lead into a conversation something like you and I have a lot in common I used to curse like you…..I counted 15 curse words in your last paragraph, you want to know what happed to me and why I don't cruses anymore………testimony time you're on…… God change my life one day here is what happened……..give them your testimony and at the end of it say to them you want to change your life forever………would you like to invite the Lord Jesus into your heart as your lord and personal savior….?

Key factor here is……..if you are rejected and told no, praise the lord………..you did what you were supposed to do……you shared, and your one step closer to a yes. Never give up remember they have to hear the message on average 7.2 times.

7.5 SHARING BY EXAMPLE WHEN THEY HANG OUT WITH YOU

Another method is to lead by example.......if anyone hangs out with you they Go to Sunday School and Church on Sunday no exceptions, no negotiations, your house your rules. At your house after supper the TV is turned off and you share a bible story with them, in your car....... the only music played is Christian music, you ask them if you can buy them a present if they say yes take them to the Christian book store buy the a cross necklace, or a study-bible if you can afford it, or a cool wrist band. If they say no, say my dime I was going to buy you a really cool cross necklace.......at least let me pray for you if I can't give you a gift.

And pull off the side of the roadway and pour out your heart to god about them, even to the point of tears it will let them see you are serious about God and who he is, and especially what you believe as they *"hear-you-pray"* this is good for them to hear.

Wear a rubber bracelet on your writs that says "Prayer Warrior" or something catchy you come up with, and when someone asks what it says or means.....bingo your stage is set...........Wearing a Christian tee shirt accomplishes this also.....Use your own mind to come up with anything, to allow the opportunity to share. Be very mindful where you share, meaning you need to exercise judgment, some places are not appropriate......example if you're on your way to a business meeting in a corporation, and you do not have enough time......you're in a two minute walk.....ask them to go to lunch with you to expand on this discussion......sorry I drifted off the subject here a little.

Remember you may be the closest thing to "Jesus" some people ever see.......In other words you use any and every tool you can think of to share, you can be very creative here, at the same time do not overdo it......the corporate work world is a very precarious place and this can require **very careful** deliberation on your part.

Be **aware** you can cause other brothers and sisters to stumble, especially if they are very early or very shallow in their relationship with the Lord. Also remember, others who do not have a relationship with the Lord may see you as a "fanatic" or "extremist" and even though you never intended to drive them away.....too much material at your desk

/ cubicle can and may cause others to stumble away or actually drive them away from Christianity......Some Christians have shared with me they wanted no part of Christianity at first because they saw a (guy/gal) at work with all this "stuff" on their desk, and they did not want to be like them.......All I am saying here is the corporate work world is a very precarious place and this can require **very careful** deliberation on your part....! And every pastor in the entire world just "**screamed**" out loud....I know!

At home at you own personal desk......Go for it.....! When someone comes to your home......even to use your bathroom......even on the vanity it should have some reminder of who God is......A sign that says prayer warrior, or scripture verse etc.......Go for it in your home.....!

7.6   SHARING VIA THE INVITATION

Another way is to simply invite someone to church. Believe me you're not going to die. Most of the people that come to church are there........ because they were invited by someone. Human fact.....we all.....like to have an open invitation with a choice to decide for ourselves....."Go" or "No-Go"....... but we like choice(s) in our American society. Invite someone to church every week, I promise you.......you will not die.

Invite people to "check out" you're churches website... if you have one. I would send this to their personal email....ask them for their personal email. Then copy & paste the churches web site in the email, so they don't have to write it down.

Invite people to any and all church functions especially fun ones like....... "Spring Golf Tournaments" and "Lady's SPA day"...!!!

Invite people to you Home.....tell them it is for the purpose of..... fun/food/fellowship. When they are there.....during the fellowship part ask them if you can share you testimony with them......It's a good idea to have other Christian friends over and have them share too.....!

7.7   SHARING BY MEDIA

I have a lady in my Sunday school class that was confined to a wheel chair since she was in her twenties, and she is "on-line" speaking and chatting with others in wheel chairs that will listen to her much more than me. This is her particular niche and she has refined it over the years. But, it could be any niche group such as......perhaps only woman's pregnancy centers or abortion blogs etc.......it could be any niche group you connect with. Just be very consistent and constant.

You could also write a book...? It may or may not make the best seller list.......but you could write a book. Write for magazine, write for a Christian magazine.....this would be great......or start your own local Christian magazine if you have the time talents and expertise.

I am not a big advocate of this but some people who have short hair can get their ears pierced and wear a cross ear ring (small and conservative) and if anyone says anything about it.......say as my lord and savior was pierced through both hand and his feet for my sins.....I wear this as a reminder of how precious it is to be a saved...knowing he will never leave me or forsake me.......would you like to invite Jesus into your heart as your lord and savior......? Even if only one person gets saved it's worth it. Do not confuse this one.....I am **not** saying if you have short hair get your ear pierced........I am saying share in any way that works for you......If my dad (age 80) and his hair is very short....... got his ear pierced, well this may not be **his** best and most advantageous opportunity to share! So when I say share via the media......think of ways to share to more than just one person.

I say share in a way that works for you.......in your favor.....when you're in the media arena.........let the people know that your core being is based on a love "relationship" with the lord Jesus.

Face book, My space, Personal email.......make it work for you when you're at home. This is a great way to use the media to share with others. This also gives you the creativity to use your own personal flare to share. God likes variety!

God wants you to give your **own person flare to share**.

8. What do I work on next

8.1 Adding VIRTUE to your faith

In the event you have made it to this point consider **adding** some very special things to your faith in accordance to the bible. Remember this the bible is not a cafeteria plan you don't pick and choose what you like or dislike, it is the living breathing word of God, infallible and basic instructions before leaving earth. It is a **holy** bible.

The first thing you should add to your faith is…….are you ready for this…….you actually will need to add something to your faith…... here we go. 1st thing is VIRTUE. What do you mean by that? Notice that here virtue is simply this……..moral integrity based on the biblical statues and commandments. I want to show you the definition of Virtue in most dictionaries they say something like:

- 1 a : conformity to a standard of right : morality
  b : a particular moral excellence
  2 plural :an order of angels — see celestial hierarchy
  3 : a beneficial quality or power of a thing
  4 : manly strength or courage : valor
  5 : a commendable quality or trait : merit
  6 : a capacity to act : potency
  7 : chastity especially in a woman

So when the bible says add to your faith   Virtue God means moral excellence and a standard of right and wrong based on the biblical principles set forth by God above. This means you have to become intimately familiar with God's laws and I highly recommend a journey through the New Testament, but just make sure you decisions are based on the biblical principles, not based on a worldly view.

Example sometimes I am so concerned about my own well being, but not others......in the state of California they have made it legal for same sex marriages. The way I vote depends on the moral views of the candidates, and a marriage according to the bible is between a man and a woman the way God designed it, not man and multiple women etc......there should be no exceptions, no negotiations, no tolerance. I should never vote on an issue to discontinue or change the bigamy law......it is morally sound and good. This is the kind of virtue you should *"guard your heart"* against the world from trying to create a tolerance for.

God wants you to add **Virtue** to your faith!

8.2   ADDING KNOWLEDGE TO YOUR FAITH

The second thing you need to add to your faith is
KNOWLEDGE. Listen to what most dictionaries say something like this for the definition of knowledge it's actually pretty good:

- 1 obsolete : cognizance
  2 a (1) : the fact or condition of knowing something with familiarity gained through experience or association (2) : acquaintance with or understanding of a science, art, or technique b (1) : the fact or condition of being aware of something (2) : the range of one's information or understanding <answered to the best of my knowledge> c : the circumstance or condition of apprehending truth or fact through reasoning

The answer lies within here........the bible is a book of books, and the answers to life are within the covers of the book, sometimes God reveals them through the stories of the Israelites, and sometimes just as a matter of fact straight out. Example in the New Testament where it tells us straight out.......we well be judged for every idle word and not to curse. 1ˢᵗ Peter 1:15 But as he which hath called you is holy, so be ye holy in **all manner of conversation**; and of course Matthew 12:36 But I say unto you, That every idle word that men shall speak, they shall give account thereof in the day of judgment. Straight forward and nothing left for wondering or pondering.

So back to knowledge how do you add this to your faith…..you keep your heart and mind open to the scriptures and try and approach the bible with this attitude……..I can't wait to see what God has to teach me today. 2nd Peter 3:18 But grow in grace, and [**in**] the **knowledge** of our Lord and Saviour Jesus Christ. To him [be] glory both now and for ever. Amen.

So try your best to learn and grow more in the knowledge of Jesus Christ. This occurs by reading the passage of scripture three times through. 1st get the big picture of what is happening, who the characters are, what they are doing, and the general place or culture in the scene. 2nd what is the story God is teaching the Israelites, and 3rdly what is the one correct interpretation God is teaching you in your own life.

How can you weave this biblical truth into the fabric of your own individual life and make it a part of the core being of who you are.

God wants you to add **knowledge** of Jesus Christ to your faith!

8.3 ADDING TEMPERANCE TO YOUR FAITH

The Third thing you need to add to your faith is TEMPERANCE. And if you're like me your thinking where have I heard that term before and what exactly does it mean again. Let's just simple look at what most dictionaries say something like:

1 : moderation in action, thought, or feeling : restraint

2 a: habitual moderation in the indulgence of the appetites or passions

b : moderation in or abstinence from the use of alcoholic beverages.

Does this strike a nerve with you……to be even keel as "they say"……try not to be a character that is either at a roller coaster high or in the lowest valley…….be even keel. Do not be a drama queen some have said…….try and be very steady and have control of your attitudes and emotions "*in-check*" not being someone that flies off the handle at the least little thing that comes your way.

Being in control and aware of what power you have to actually change the impact of any given situation and what it means in the grand scheme of things. This requires help from God above and you will need to be in prayer about this one, especially if you struggle with this one.

Let me interject one important piece of scripture here again......
Philippians 2:14-15 Do all things without murmurings and disputing(s): That ye may be blameless and harmless, the sons of God, without rebuke, in the midst of a crooked and perverse nation, among whom ye shine as lights in the world;

Notice here that it says "**ALL**" things without murmurings and disputing.......be optimistic and find something good in all the bad.........when you speak let it be an encouragement and uplifting to others.........remember *anyone* can complain, but...you be the **light** that shines through the darkness ....of an otherwise gloomy situation.......be **optimistic** the rest of your life from this moment forward.

You **let** your light shine by finding something good to say today. Be well balance and optimistic in heart always having Temperance added to your faith.

God wants you to add **temperance** to your faith!

8.4   ADDING PATIENCE TO YOUR FAITH

The fourth thing you need to add to your faith is
PATIENCE. And if you're like me you need to take this one to heart. The original term is so much more descriptive it's "***Longsuffering***" and that "*fits-like-a-glove*" for most of us.

How do you add patience to your faith, slow down and try for once "*not to be in a hurry*" it will actually shock you if you are able to perform a task without this time pressing constraint. Some of you who work in project management will be amazed if you slow down and........do one task at a time with precision............how much more fluid the entire process**s.......** seem to go.

Do one task at a time slowly and do that one task really well, then move on. Have you ever read an email you sent in a hurry and left out some very important words.........this takes you down a notch on the confidence scale.

I would like to talk longer on this issue but I am in a hurry......
stop-it! Patience is learned **not granted**, and patience requires **work** on your part.

Want more patience, work slower, harder, smarter, and realize it will be learned over time, patience is not a quick fix.

God wants you to add **patience** to your faith!

8.5   ADDING GODLINESS TO YOUR FAITH

The fifth thing you need to add to your faith is GODLINESS. How on earth do you add Godliness to your faith? As a matter of fact what are we calling godliness that is really an unobtainable goal correct?

This is a study of the Greek word *eusebeia*, used in the New Testament to express the idea of inner piety, spiritual maturity, or godliness. In TITUS 1:1, the Apostle Paul states that he is an apostle of Jesus Christ according to the criterion of the faith of the chosen people of God who have a full and applied knowledge of the truth which is the standard for godliness. So what do we really mean by Godliness via in the layman terms what exactly are we talking about here?

Godliness is being able to walk with God daily, **applying** the biblical principles to the way you live your life, and the decisions you make "*day-to-day*", and giving honor and glory to God in the highest, making God the center focus of your life.

Applying the biblical principles of the bible to the way you live your life is a mark of spiritual maturity. You see....the big difference between being a "*hearer*" of the word of God.....and a being a "*doer*" of the word of God.

God wants you to add **godliness** to your faith!

8.6   ADDING BROTHERLY KINDNESS TO YOUR FAITH

The sixth thing you need to add to your faith is BROTHERLY KINDNESS. How is kindness different from brotherly kindness? Here is how it's different.......you will be courteous or polite to be kind, but brotherly kindness is spending resources and time to be a part of your brothers / sisters world.

Brotherly kindness means going the extra mile to make sure your brother's needs are met and your brother is squared away. The key here is expecting **nothing.......** in return, working towards looking after your bother's needs and then moving onward.......did I stress looking for nothing , not even a "**thank-you**" in return!!!!

Kindness you see..........has a way of coming back around to you.......especially if you ask for nothing in return, especially a courtesy thank-you (don't even expect it). **True kindness asks for nothing in return**.

Brotherly kindness should be an unselfish act for another brother's well being, not your own personal agenda and reward system. Some people get so caught up in how they define brotherly kindness it prohibits them from the act itself.

In other words, if a brother fails to say "*thank-you*" or some other courtesy etiquette rule is lacking.......the person extending the kindness is **all** bent out of shape, frustrated and wishes not to be kind again. **Wrong**, who knows you heart.......God sees right through the human flaws and sees the heart and mind .....And trust me on this one.............God knows if you are authentic or not.

Be real......and extend brotherly kindness, out of the goodness in your heart. This way you will actually let your light shine and people can see Christ in you..........Did Christ every scold anyone for........ **not saying** thank-you......or some other etiquette rule..........People can see Christ in you if you are being......kind without constraints, especially when you are extending brotherly kindness.

Some of you would say well.......God made me who I am....... and being kind is not my nature. Drop to your knees and ask God to change you, like he changed you when you first got saved! Read it one more time the bible (authority) word of God says in 2nd Peter 5-7 to Add brotherly kindness to your faith. Please allow God to work in you, and through you.....be the salt and light to the world and one way is by being just like Christ.......extend "brotherly kindness" as he did to you. Let your light shine, by extending "brotherly kindness"!

God wants you to add **brotherly kindness** to your faith!

8.7   ADDING CHARITY TO YOUR FAITH

The seventh thing you need to add to your faith is
CHARITY. Sometimes when we see this term we automatically think of giving to a.......not-for-profit "organization". The term should not be confused with the more modern term that is totally restricted to mean

benevolent giving. All of us get this term confused occasionally with benevolent giving of some kind because there are so many not-for-profit organizations out there.

So what is CHARITY......? Charity is the badge of a Christian, the one glaring and distinguishing feature that says I am a follower of Christ. Charity is unconditional love and compassion for the brethren both the saved and the unsaved. Read this *"really read it"* and think long and hard before you use the term "Christian" and your name with this title..........1ˢᵗ Corinthians 13 Paul's Letter to the Corinthians........ Though I speak with the tongues of men and of angels, and have not charity, I am become [as] sounding brass, or a tinkling cymbal. And though I have [the gift of] prophecy, and understand all mysteries, and all knowledge; and though I have all faith, so that I could remove mountains, and have not charity, I am nothing. And though I bestow all my goods to feed [the poor], and though I give my body to be burned, and have not charity, it profiteth me nothing. Charity suffereth long, [and] is kind; charity envieth not; charity vaunteth not itself, is not puffed up, Doth not behave itself unseemly, seeketh not her own, is not easily provoked, thinketh no evil; Rejoiceth not in iniquity, but rejoiceth in the truth; Beareth all things, believeth all things, hopeth all things, endureth all things. Charity never faileth: but whether [there be] prophecies, they shall fail; whether [there be] tongues, they shall cease; whether [there be] knowledge, it shall vanish away. For we know in part, and we prophesy in part. But when that which is perfect is come, then that which is in part shall be done away. When I was a child, I spake as a child, I understood as a child, I thought as a child: but when I became a man, I put away childish things. For now we see through a glass, darkly; but then face to face: now I know in part; but then shall I know even as also I am known. And now abideth faith, hope, charity, these three; but the greatest of these [is] charity.

2ⁿᵈ Peter 5-8: And beside this, giving all diligence, add to your faith virtue; and to virtue knowledge; And to knowledge temperance; and to temperance patience; and to patience godliness; And to godliness brotherly kindness; and to brotherly kindness charity. For if these things be in you, and abound, they make [you that ye shall] neither [be] barren nor unfruitful in the knowledge of our Lord Jesus Christ.

God wants you to add **charity** to your faith........!

8.8   SPIRITUAL WAREFARE

When you begin to make an effort to become a Christian you come under attack, spiritually speaking. How so, the bible tells us so, that we will wrestle (have difficulty dealing with) worldly issues. Ephesians 6:12 For we wrestle not against flesh and blood, but against principalities, against powers, against the rulers of the darkness of this world, against spiritual wickedness in high [places]. So you see we will come under attack and the demonic forces work and wait patiently for very specific temptations design especially for you. What tempts one man may not be a temptation for another man. We are all different. So who tempts us......invisible spirits that make you think 1-they don't exist 2- it was all your idea, 3-they cloak and minimize the consequences of sin.

Notice James 1:13-16 Let no man say when he is tempted, I am tempted of God: for God cannot be tempted with evil, neither tempteth he any man: But every man is tempted, when he is drawn away of his own lust, and enticed. Then when lust hath conceived, it bringeth forth sin: and sin, when it is finished, bringeth forth death. Do not err, my beloved brethren.........this is simply saying we are drawn away by our own lust very seductively. Example for economic reason s a guy ask his girl friend to *"move-in"* with him.....during the course of time he and she find they are really not compatible as a couple and they don't really like each other all that much she accidently gets pregnant and they decide to have an abortion and end their relationship shortly thereafter. Has this ever happened to anyone out there or have you ever been a part of this.

See how you or they lived out James 1 13-16. James 1:12 comes into play Blessed [is] the man that endureth temptation: for when he is tried, he shall receive the crown of life, which the Lord hath promised to them that love him. The temptation is to rush right into a relationship and not think anything through, just simply listen to the world and go with the old saying you never know somebody until you *"live-with-them"*.

In all fairness the man woman relationship is very complex and should be carefully *"thought-out"* and given **much** prayer and consideration........If you both do not go to the same church or you both are from different denominations you should not be unequally yoked together.......this is should be the very first issue.......you ever work out as a couple before you rush into a relationship........from there go to marriage counselors prior to marriage and discuss how financial transactions will be handled, and many other issues..........Family management and spending money.......is an issue that must and should be worked through as a couple, otherwise this can lead to the downfall of a marriage quickly.

Anyway, my point here is we all come under attack one way or another. Spiritual warfare really exists.

We all come under persecution and this is in a variety of forms...... could be worldly attacks from other groups of people, or individual attacks from one person, or in the form of afflictions such as health issues, that keep you from worshiping.

Sometimes afflictions may be that God needs to develop character integrity within you.....? I don't really have the answer to personal health issue that occurs to each individual. All I know is this.....If I can bring honor and glory to God, and I have to suffer in order to do so...... as painful as it is......so mote it be.....and to God be the glory.

The Lord Jesus had to suffer greatly for all of us, physically, intellectually, emotionally, and spiritually. Without the shedding of blood the human cannot be forgiven for sins physically, intellectually, emotionally, and spiritually.

Even the blood speaks to God....remember when God ask Cain why does your brother's blood *"cry out"* to me from the ground.....?.

2nd Timothy 3:12 Yea, and **all** that will live godly in Christ Jesus shall suffer persecution.

I want to share my personal diary with you from the summer of 2010 when I was writing this book................I never understand the "**why**" in life, I only know God is Good, All the time. The "**why**" is not really important to me, because God's ways are not my ways and I claim this scripture.......Romans 8:28 and we know that all things work together for good to them that love God, to them who are called according to his purpose.

In other words the "**why**" is not important, my relationship with God is important!

God wants you to "**give-up**" on the "**why**"

9. EPILOGUE

I am reminded here of the word of God where in 2nd Timothy 3:12 Yea, and all that will live godly in Christ Jesus shall **suffer** persecution.

Sometimes this comes in a variety of forms and shapes. Look for the ways you can bring glory to God on high.......no matter what the circumstances.

The book actually ends here, I have enclosed my cancer diary, for those who have ever gone through or about to go through cancer treatments. I did not disclose the real names of the doctors.

I was told I had cancer in on July 6th 2010 and the doctor did not know the source of my cancer. Therefore; I kept a journal of my "dark days" where I underwent 35 radiation treatments, (6) six-hour chemo therapy treatments, and "radical neck dissection" surgery. I kept a diary for this and post it here as the epilogue. It is very personal and representative of the dark days I went through with my cancer treatments.

9.1 SUMMER OF 2010 CANCER DIARY FOR DALE L. ELLIOTT

2010_24_May Towards the end of May I remember riding my "motorcycle-in" to work one day and thinking wow it's hot this morning, not the normal cool chill it takes your body a minute or two just to get "*used-to-it*".......no it was hot and muggy riding in to work. As I revved up to 60 miles per hour the cool wind was actually refreshing this morning. The temperature had gotten up and over 90 degrees several afternoons now for about the last couple of weeks and I notice my throat was sore. I had ***reluctantly*** scheduled a doctor's appointment; however, on the day of my appointment I was talking to a Julie (a wonderful co-worker) and as I turned my head to one side I notice a slight lump in my throat on the right side. When I arrived at the doctor's office I told him about this and he put me on antibiotics and told me to come back and see him in about two weeks he was concerned about the swollen lymph node, said it is probably a viral infection of some kind.

2010_07_June When I returned to my doctor after two weeks of antibiotics the sore throat was dissipating, but the lump was still there so he told me to go down stairs and have a CT scan. I did that very day and he called me a couple of days later and sent me to an "Ears/Nose/Throat" specialist.....Dr. "G" set up a needle biopsy and this was like (4) hornets stinging me in my neck, but after the shot for numbness, the rest of the procedure was all was down hill. Dr. "G" wanted me to come to his office on June 30th, but I had another appointment. Dr. "G" met with me on Tuesday July 6th instead of June 30th.

2010_06_July Announcement   My prognosis was "squamous cell carcinoma" **cancer**. Dr. "G" put a scope through my nose and down my throat and found some dark spots on my tongue and said this could be the source of the cancer. He proceeded to tell me I could have surgery or chemo therapy but I should definitely undergo both. Since he could not locate the source he wanted to do a biopsy of the back of my tongue, so I said can we do this now. (2) days later we did.

2010_07_July Prayer Meeting Dale Speaks Out   Bishop Brian (my pastor not too fond of the title I call him by) gave a brief service on why good things happen to bad people and bad things happened to good people and then he ask if anyone had any special prayer request........with my heart pounding, and very nervously I announce to my church family on Wednesday night at pray meeting that I needed special prayer....I had cancer and the doctor did not really know the source it was "squamous cell carcinoma". As soon as I said this a man in front of me turned around and said I had that twelever years ago, I will talk to you after this, a lady turned around and said I had that 2 or 3 years ago…..my heart and my counterance was lifted up that very moment…..how we need our church family. My men's group prayed with me, my close friends (Ray, Alfred, David) prayed with me, and Bishop Brian prayed with me. Later that night Mom & Dad prayed with me…….over the phone, and my sister prayed with me over the phone, my sister also put me on her Sunday school prayer list, and put me on cousin Connie's prayer list.

2010_08_July Michele's Email to Sunday School-Class   For those of you that were at the prayer service last night you heard the story. For those of you that were not, please do not feel slighted…..right now as I type this it has only been just over 36 hours since we learned of this. *"On Tuesday Dale went to the doctor to get the results of a test that he thought was just a routine check for his sore throat. Well, the doctor advised him that the results of the test showed that he has Squamous cell carcinoma (SCC) in his Lymph nodes on the right side of his neck. While this type of cancer is not as fatal as many other forms of cancer, the concern the doctor had was that they did not know the source of the cancer in his lymph node. He asked Dale if he had any irritation in his throat or any other issues that he could think of and Dale said "Well my sinuses have really been draining lately". So the doctor ran a scope/camera thru his nose to his throat to see if he could see anything right there in the office. He told Dale that he thought he saw something on the very back of his tongue and that he would like to do a biopsy. Dale said "If you can do it now, let's do it". Needless to say the doctor got a laugh out of that and he said, let's see what we can do. They called us on Wednesday around 1:00 and scheduled the biopsy for Friday. Then at 3:00 they called us back and said they had a cancellation for Thursday so we were moved to Thursday. So, we head to church in a daze and Dale says to me…….."I am just going to talk to Brian in private" He did not want to really talk to anyone about it. So because I had already agreed to help out in the nursery, I went and did that and Dale went to the prayer service. Well, for those of you that have read the lesson it is about David and courage. That lesson was really on Dale's heart in the prayer service and he said he was overcome with the thought that it takes courage to stand up and tell people what was going on with him/us So he slowly raised his hand when Brian asked for prayer requests and told everyone. God provided people immediately to Dale that had experienced the exact same cancer that he has and they provided great encouragement to him. Thanks to everyone for the prayers. They really meant a lot to both of us. Dale left church Wednesday feeling encouraged and with less anxiety than when he arrived. So today bright and early Dale and I head to TMH and Dale had the surgery. It took longer than expected and the emotions of it all just kept overwhelming me. I kept praying and reading God's word and I personally want to thank everyone for their prayers. Finally the doctor came and spoke to me after the surgery and he was amazed. He told me that the spot on his tongue that he thought was the source was not cancer. He checked several areas of it and it was not the source of the cancer, so he decided to continue looking. He said finally he saw this little bitty speck......mind you he spent nearly 1 minute telling me how small this spot was. He really could not believe how small it was. The spot is on his throat near his carotid artery. He did a biopsy of the spot and sure enough that is the source. He told me it was really amazing that they caught this so early. He said that this cancer is rarely caught early because of its location. He told me that usually when he sees this type it is well advanced and the treatment is very severe. However he kept restating how amazed he was at finding the source so early. I said it is a miracle. Dale is home now, sleeping off all of the meds. He is not suppose to talk a lot for the next day or so (hahahahaha), so do not be offended if he does not call you/returns calls right away. We have radiation treatment and possibly chemo to look forward to for his treatment but we are so thankful that God revealed this lump in Dale's throat and that he revealed the source of the cancer to our doctor today. It really is overwhelming to think of what has happened here and the miracle of finding the source of this cancer today. Thank you all so much for the prayers. We thank God for all of you".*

As you can imagine, I can't think about anything else, but on that Wednesday night as soon as I announced it, one man Andy turned around (I was sitting right in front of him) and he said I had that (12) years ago, I'll talk to you about this, and Judy said I had that 2-3 years ago, I'll talk to you too. God will work in your life if you will let him. Then we split into groups of men and women and the men prayed for me and another Sunday school teacher Brain who had been diagnosed with prostate cancer. It seems unreal and I was having trouble wrapping my mind around what was happening. I was told I had cancer on Tuesday July 06, 2010......On Wednesday morning, I called my mom from work and told her what had transpired within the past 24 hours, and through her tears she told me to have a really good attitude about this. We were both crying when I hung up.

2010_08_July_Deacon Gilmore   A newly ordained deacon "Deacon *Gilmore*", came to visit me and brought me popsicles (yeah)......he went out of his way to visit me at 3:00 the day of my biopsy, and I was awaken by Michele and met with him and visited in our living room. We prayed and he left after a brief visit around 3:00 PM.....he told me he fell asleep praying for me the night before. What a wonderful visit from my Christian brother.

2010_13_Julie wonderful co-worker God never stops working in your life   Julie said the sweetest prayer for me in my office at work, I can't recall a more eloquently put prayer off the top of her head....it was wonderful. Here is the email from JZ my co-worker: *Dale, Dan and I would like to fast one day a week for you during your radiation treatment. Please let us know if there is a better day to fast than another. I guess I was trying to line it up on a one of the days you get treatment but I know it doesn't matter. I know our prayer will be heard either way. If there is a fasting list from your church we can get on, feel free to send our info their way. We did this for one of our pastors during the last (3) months of a very scary pregnancy such that someone was fasting for them every day. Standing with you,*
Julie (and Dan)

Wow God puts the right people in your life at the right time........how I need to hear a prayer and that was a very uplifting email that boosted my counterance.

2010_14_July Dr. "B" I had a 1:30 meeting with Dr. "B" to discuss radiation treatment. He said they would give me radiation on both sides of my neck and I would probably have some permanent side effects. A lot of this depends on how my body responds to radiation. I will probably lose some saliva wetness and experience some dryness, and may not have to shave my neck ever again. He did a consult for one and ½ hours..... answered all our questions....I have to go for 35 treatments, 7-weeks, M-F. Then I will have to do a consult with the "*chemo-people*" and see if they are going to give me a small dose of chemo-therapy, which I would like just to make sure it kills everything. Dr. "B" put that black hose through my nose and down my throat….very uncomfortable and he saw the same tumor on the base of my tongue that Dr. "G" saw…….and Michele told him this was not the source, but he said don't worry they are very close together, the radiation will kill all the abnormal cells. This was Wednesday, today 07-15-2010 I go back to Dr. "B" and he gives me an IV-CT scan and begins measuring the area of my neck where he will give me radiation. He will also make the necessary arrangements with the "chemo-people" and I will have an upcoming appointment with them. I spoke with Bonnie (pastor's wife wonderful lady and former cancer survivor) last night at church and she told me God is in control, you are just along for the ride, and when she gave up the fight, the worry, the fear of the unknowns, and "let-go" only then could she get to the place of intimacy with God and begin to grow. She had a terrible bout with cancer they sent her home to die 15 years ago. I spoke with Mom, and she said to have a good attitude about this and thanked-me for updating her, and she reminded me………mother and daddy are praying for me and her new pastor Whiten said he would pray for me. I Spoke with Sandy too…….she is using the spreadsheet I sent her. My thoughts as of yesterday, pray for God's perfect will not his permissive will in accordance to our prayers. Here is what I am thinking about: God **always** has a plan, and within this plan be aware there are two parts here.

1st God's perfect will (God's way that is perfect) and achieves God's plan flawlessly.

2nd God's permissive will (God's can allow his will to be accomplished by other routes)

God will have…….."his will"…….done either by Route A, or Route B, but either way God's will is going to be accomplished, however through the *"prayers-of-his-people"* he may allow a different route to be taken that still accomplishes God's will. (Permissive Will). So tread lightly here make sure you are in the will of God and understand what is at stake when you pray Dale Elliott. Julie and I had the conversation earlier today at work about God's will and permissive will. I can't wait to meet with the "chemo-people" and get the show on the road. "OCD is kicking in, I am impatient but trying to work on it….come on let's go! (Maybe I need more work)

2010_15_July Dr. "B" I had a 3:30 Appointment with Dr. "B", what a trip here is what happened. They put me in a room and I had blood drawn from my left hand, (I could not look) and then an "IV-Set-up" was installed when I finally looked down, she had to stick me twice (that felt like a big hornet stinging me) and then I was led into a room where a girl name Brandi made me change into a gown from the waist up, and then she lead me to another room for the "CT-Scan" process. A girl name Lani came to meet Brandi and I…….she told me she was from the local college FSU in the music program and ask me to fill out a survey (1) page, and she ask me what kind of music I liked as she would be playing a guitar and singing during the procedure, if I did not object to this. I told her I like Christian music and ask her if she had any Chris Tomlin or Steven Curtis Chapman music. She did not have them but she had some Christian music, and she could play some Eddie Van Halen if she ran out of material, or my procedure ran longer than expected at my request…of course. I was then laid down on the CT scan (movable) table, given a brace for my knees to ease the *"pain/pressure"* on my back, and then they told me to be *"very"* still. The doctor came in and wrote on my ear, neck, and chest with a marker to lay out the areas for measurement. The Dr. and the Physicist decided I would not need to shave off the "French –beard" aka "GOE-Tee" or have a mouth piece….whatever that means. I had a watery mesh mask from the top of my head to just below my shoulder line put on me then it was clamped down on me very tight and it started shrinking to the contours of my face as I was moving back and forth through a CT scanner and the girl was playing Christian music over the loud speaker and singing. Then the IV kicked in…….and I felt warm and a slightly burning sensation as the dye went in…..and this continued along with the mask getting stiffer and tighter as I was moving in and out of this really huge…..doughnut like machine, I could hear the guitar and singing in the background along with the major sounds of the machine………..it really was quite loud and the claustrophobia was actually getting to me (I am **not** claustrophobic), with minor *"difficulty"* I was able to endure the 30 minute experience. Then I was unmasked, (un-"IV"-ed), and given a card to meet with the *"chemo-people"* (different doctors) and scheduled for the 1st of 35 radiation treatments. I went home and kissed Michele (wife), briefly petted Kaya (dog), and cut the front and back yard 2 ½ hours on the lawnmower before the thunderstorm and lighting begin. What an evening for me........have mercy.

2010_16_July Friday Men's Breakfast Les was diagnosed as being a diabetic and he did not eat he will be trying to lose 50 lbs and cutting back on his caloric intake. Rolland gave a good and brief devotion about when God puts someone on your mind through the Holy Spirit and brings this thought upon you, that you should either call or pray for that person as soon as possible, and then he spoke about the Judgment House and to be very mindful about your destiny and destination. The men prayed for me and lifted me up in prayer concerning my radiation treatments, and the testimony to come out of this bout with cancer. Brian is who I sat beside has prostate cancer and will be undergoing surgery within the next couple of weeks to remove his prostrate, but he offered up a very soothing and uplifting prayer for me as did the other men at the table. I prayed to God about being a wonderful and mighty God, and thanked him for his mercy and grace first, then I prayed for the lord to hear the words of the men at the table and be with us all as spiritual leaders in the home, and for our unspoken request, and our hearts and minds to be in conformity to God's will not try to bend our own will to meet God's will, but to actually accept and be a participant of God's will in our life, and to be with our upcoming Judgment House ministry in the fall.

2010_18_July Sunday Afternoon Prison Ministry   I had never been to this before but God was dealing with me and I wanted to be biblical and actually visit those in prison, so I contacted one of the men at my church who is a part of prison ministry. Turns out, this is a very organized event with an agenda and schedule. They wanted me to commit to (4) intense days of program, however; because of the cancer treatments, and work I could not attend during the days, so I will only be able to attend on Saturday and possibly Sunday. Anyway the men there learned I had cancer through one of my friends and (3) other men....have had cancer there....... they are survivors, and they spoke to me, and before we left all the men prayed for me, several of them laid hands on me like my Sunday school class did, and we all prayed at the same time (never had done this before) and then we transitioned from the prayer to a song, (Jesus there is something about that name) and we left. It was different and uplifting. Later unfortunately Michele and I had to call my buddy John and tell him due to doctors orders I am not supposed to be around many people especially ones in populations like a jail......not to mentioned how bad I was feeling after chemo and radiation, so I canceled the prison ministry this year.

2010_19_July Monday Morning email from Michele to our Sunday School Class   many of you heard after church yesterday that Bonnie was in the hospital. We have learned that she has meningitis. They are not sure what kind it is and will not find out until Tuesday. Because of this, they are treating her with antibiotics for the worst case scenario. This means that she will not be able to see people because of the possibility she may be contagious. They are treating her now with masks on. Stephanie spoke with Linda last night and she advised that they are asking for no calls to Bonnie's cell phone and no visits right now. I spoke and prayed with her last night and she was in great spirits. She told me she has had some really good quiet time with the Lord. I told her that that those caretakers were in store for some great blessings because God is going to use her in great ways. Please pray for her treatment and for her strength and of course for the family to be comforted and strengthened during this time. Many of you also know that Natalie will be going in for surgery tomorrow on her shoulder. I told Natalie and Chuck yesterday that we wanted to set up meals for them, but they advised that they had "Moms" coming to take care of them for the next two weeks. Please pray for the doctors that will be treating Natalie. We all know she has been in great pain since December. Also pray for Chuck and the family to have strength and comfort during this time. When we find out about visitors and calls after the surgery we will let you know. Lastly Dale thanks everyone for the prayers. He feels them daily and is in such a good place to begin his treatments on Thursday. We cannot thank you all enough for the prayers. I personally am thankful that he has a peace about him during this time.

2010_19_July Monday Morning Phone Call to Wakulla court system I called the Wakulla court house where I had been summoned for jury duty. I spoke with the lady, and told her I was a cancer patient undergoing treatment, she was empathetic asking me when I should be through with treatment I told her around September 10th assuming all goes well. She said ok, and my civil duties will be deferred until such a time I can serve 12-14-2010. She is going to send me another notice at the beginning of December to remind me. So the blessing is I will serve my county respectively in December 2010, but I do not have to miss any work this month for which I am grateful. My doctor appointments have been scheduled in the afternoon, after 3 PM. Currently, I work for 7AM to 3PM. I am praying for a reoccurring appointment for radiation at 3:30 PM.

2010_21_July Wednesday at 04:15 Appointment with Doctor "G"   I spoke with Dr. "G" and he said this was the result to the biopsy.........I have a tumor the size of a small pea next to my "carotid artery" that is the source of cancer it is HPV in nature. Dr. "B" (radiation doctor) took a scope camera and he saw a dark spot aka tumor that Dr. "B" saw as being a marble size growth not intended to be there. Anyway back to Dr. "G", the HPV cancer responds very well to radiation treatment and chemo therapy. This was good news for me. Dr."G" said after the radiation and perhaps chemo therapy he would allow 4-6 weeks and then surgery as a "clean-up" type of surgery to remove the right side chain of lymph nodes. So the good news my HPV cancer responds good to radiation & chemo therapy.......bad news I still have to have surgery to remove the one chain of lymph nodes. Here are some general facts about the HPV cancer the origin is: .:"HPV — WHO GETS IT? Human papillomavirus (HPV) affects both females and males. HPV transmission can happen with any kind of genital contact with someone who has HPV—intercourse isn't necessary. Many people who have HPV don't even know it, because the virus often has no signs or symptoms. That means you can get the virus or pass it on to your partner without knowing it. In the United States, an estimated 75% to 80% of males and females will be infected with HPV in their lifetime. For most, the virus will clear on its own, but when it doesn't, HPV can have consequences: And there is no way to predict who will or won't

clear the virus. There are about 6 million new cases of genital HPV*
in the United States each year. It's estimated that 74% of them occur
in 15- to 24-year-olds". So in other words I may have contracted this
virus that turned into cancer somewhere in my past sinful days at
college or otherwise......there is shame, and I am reminded that the
bible rings true once again "***your sins will find you out***".......and sin
has consequences. I personally feel this is why I contracted the HPV
that eventually turned into cancer. That is my feelings on this matter,
and I am ashamed of many of the things I did in my past.....I am a
sinful man, this is true......I have asked God for forgiveness and prayed
for.......God to cleanse me for all unrighteousness........But I must tell
my family the truth......I am a sinner, ashamed for many of my past
actions, especially in college, and perhaps, this HPV cancer is unrelated
to that, nevertheless I take accountability for my actions and apologize
to my family for not keeping God's laws and commandments that way
I should have concerning........sexual purity when I was in college......
the shame is fully upon me.......as are the consequences. Romans tells
us......."we have all sinned and come short of the glory of God".......
this is especially true in my case.....I am a sinner and work every day
to **try my best** to follow God's commandments, but I tell you (my
family) the truth........I was not this way in college, and in a small part
of my childhood and adult life.........I am ashamed for many of my
actions..........ashamed and regretful, and embarrassed too.........but
I hear the scriptures ring in my head..........Press on for the mark and
the higher calling of God. And it is my own wife Michele that reminds
me of the God's word as she ends her emails with this: "Do not call to
mind the former things, Or ponder things of the past. Behold, I will
do something new, Now it will spring forth; Will you not be aware of
it? I will even make a roadway in the wilderness, Rivers in the desert.
The beasts of the field will glorify Me, The jackals and the ostriches,
Because I have given waters in the wilderness And rivers in the desert,
To give drink to My chosen people. Isaiah 43:18-20".

I love you Michele and thank-you for the encouragement you
provide me.

2010_22_July Thursday at 10:15 Appointment with Doctor "B"
My first radiation treatment wow I am nervous, but anxious to get this

underway.......Today at my work we have a bible study and Dan (Julie's husband) prayed for me, and I prayed for him, he is having temporary cloudiness like loss of vision...his primary care physician says is due to anxiety and stress. Dan raised my name up in a kind and wonderful way to the Lord.......how soothing it was to my heart. Thank-God for Christian brothers and Christian sisters.........When I arrived a girl named Melanie showed me the (3) changing rooms where I would undress from the waist up and put on a hospital gown. She then showed me another "*mini-waiting*" room, where I will go every time. Today she called me in and they put the mesh mask on me and clamped it down very tight....did some (2) x-rays in the beginning and they took a lot of measurements and markings on the outside of the mask, and they told me this would be a longer than normal day.........That mask was tight........and finally the doctor approved the measurements and the markings........seems like I was in the mask for 30 long minutes........ then they were going to make sure the "*set- up*" was to be synchronized with the computer and they will put all these settings in the radiation machine. The radiation started and this big machine made this buzzing sound like I was being "zapped" and the girls (radiation technicians) would come and check the settings measurements and tell me.......you are finished with one of three different areas they have to "treat" aka "shoot- the- radiation", aka "zap" me. I was coming close to the edge of the envelope on the claustrophobic side of things......I can tell you that mask was clamped down tight to protect other areas.......and after (1) more x-ray.......I was finally finished, (40 minutes total, I got to wear my watch), I was then escorted to the changing room where I put my shirt on, glasses on, and then I looked in the mirror.........I noticed from the top of my forehead to the base of my neck I had red waffle patter of mesh screening........I starting laughing because I looked just like an alien or some creature from outer space........ Imagine a mesh pattern on every inch of your face, ears, and neck..........I tell you I looked very funny in the mirror, I was laughing........how goofy I must have looked, and even when I got back to work the waffle pattern was just barely beginning to fade.....I tell you I looked "funny" waffle face, waffle face. God answers prayers though........right now I work at EPA as an "OPS" contractor and my hours are 7:AM to 3:PM and all future appoints are Monday through Friday 3:30 PM.......Yes God answers prayers. I do not have to miss any work so far…..God is good…….All the time………..! My dear friend Melissa in Lithia Springs, and I prayer for 3:30 time on the radiation appointment…….Michele and other may have prayed for this too……!

2010_23_July Friday 3: PM Appointment with Doctor Viral "BRO"
My meeting with the chemo doctor……I had a 3:00 appointment with the chemo doctor and a 3:30 appointment with the radiation doctor….. so I left work at 2:30 PM arrived at the chemo place at 2:45 explained the urgency of my situation with the receptionist and she passed this message on to the doctors on staff. There were a lot of sickly looking people in the waiting room, as was expected, I rode my motorcycle so I was there with a helmet, jacket and gloves……..I did not *"fit-in"* too well………After only five minutes in the waiting room the door opened and a man called my name Mr. Elliott………when I looked up I saw this 6'3" 280 lbs. giant with big hands…….I thought wow, this guy is a big worker, but maybe they have to hire people like this to help pick-up & lift certain types of patients. As we were walking back I noticed his head almost hit the ceiling, but we stopped in the maze of rooms and he said "we will have you in radiation by 3:30 PM Mr. Elliott don't worry", and shut the door. I thought wow this is a big guy in some ways reminded me of an "NFL player" once you see them in reality you realize how big they are. He had a "Learch-like" fashion about him and the way he carried himself. In some ways he reminded me of the character "Learch" on the TV series "The Adams Family". My original doctor I was scheduled was out sick today, so I would be seeing another doctor. When the door opened after a couple of minutes the same guy came in aka "Learch" and shook my hand and said Mr. Elliott I am Dr. "BRO" I will need to examine you, he had put on his stethoscope and he felt of my lymph nodes and my neck….wow his hands were enormous, and he listened to my heart beat, mashed on my sides, lungs and back asking me if I felt any pain each time…….then he said come on out lets go into my office to talk. Once I sat down he said ok, here is the way we see it, you are right on the border line of a judgment call here, so to be safe we are proactively giving you a small dosage of chemo therapy. This should help with the radiation treatments and seeing how we caught this early you should be fine. He prescribed (3) different medications and a

general nausea medicine for me. 7-weeks of being stuck one day a week with (4) hours of an "IV" that is 1 hours of pre-flush saline solution, 1-hour of medicine, and two hour of flushing out the system........I have to miss work, no arguing about this one, and take the *"rest-of-the-day"* off after this. Michele will take the next (7) Tuesdays *"off-work"* and take me to the cancer center. I was depressed when I left there on the motorcycle, but I did arrive for my 2nd radiation session on time....... and this went a lot shorter and smoother than my first treatment. The mask was tight, I could open my eyes and see this huge round armature come around with this super big round disc with a laser beam on it....... then the technicians leave the room to a control room and switch on the machine then it makes this buzzing noise like you are being zapped and then after about a minute it quits, the big round disc is repositioned and the people (2) technicians {Melanie and Krieg...last names unknown} Come in and make some fine tuning adjustments like measurements and markings on the mask, then leave and say you're doing great be real still and we will issue the 2nd treatment, they repeat this process until the third treatment is done. Then they help me up, escort me out of the room, I change and go home. Today I called Michele, informed her I was on my way.....rode the motorcycle home...over all it was a good day, but I was tired. I got up at 4:30 AM and the day was long. I took a nap and Michele and I went to hear the Dr. Ott lecture at the Crawfordville community center........on the oil spill in the "Gulf of Mexico". Dr. Ott is a toxicologist and she did the science on the Exxon Valdez oil spill. Basically we will receive the effects of this oil spill for the next 30 years, and it make take longer before our waters get back to normal. This has a severe and profound effect on the marine life. We should really think about eating seafood down here, it could have repercussion to the people. Alaska is still (21-years later) suffering from the 1989 oil spill. Alaska, commercial fishing and marine life in that area...town of "Cordova" has never recovered......1,300 miles of their surrounding coastline were affected by this....etc........bottom line is don't eat seafood caught in the Gulf for the next 30 plus years.....that is what I got out of her lecture.

Back to the cancer journal....the only side affects I have noticed is the "fatigue".....I am very tired lately. I got a card in the mail from my mother it was very sweet and said.....she and daddy are praying for me.

I got an email from my friend Melissa in Lithia Springs……..that went like this: *It's that time of day. Just said a prayer for you… Tried to call you yesterday evening. Sorry I missed you. I'm heading out of town Sunday to Myrtle Beach. Won't be back until Thursday. However, I will have my cell phone if you need me. My prayers won't stop, I can promise you that. In fact, my knees are starting to get carpet burn. :-) Next week, a lot of prayers will be going up for you as I'm standing by the ocean. I always feel so close to God when I'm there. What a perfect place to be praying for you!! Love you!! me*
Melissa

2010_27_July Tuesday 10:00 AM 1ˢᵗ Chemo Treatment
My first thought is only (7) more and I will be finished…..…yes!

Now here is what happened, I showed up at 9:45 AM and was told to go in the waiting room for about 25 minutes, where I received a couple more forms to fill out. Michele filled them out for me while I went outside to call my friend Cliff. . I have had the opportunity to pray with my buddy Clifford …how I cherish his friendship, and I miss taking lunches with him…….I really enjoyed our talks. Then a nurse volunteer came down named "Rita" and escorted us to the third floor, I had my Bible, Sunday School Lesson [teacher's addition"] to study, and the prescribed medication "Learch" aka Dr. "BRO" had written for me……….my fear of the unknown was rising and my anxiety level was up, I was very apprehensive about the next "*unknown*" step. I was not looking forward to being "*stuck/pricked*" with an "IV" needle and told to sit still for the next (4) hours…….As it turned out Michele sent out an email about this, to the entire Sunday school class asking for prayer……and the "IV" stick was not that bad, I got to wear my prescriptions sun-glasses (Costa Del Mar love them) the entire time it was very bright in that room, Michele took a picture of me in the "*recliner*" at chemo therapy, and in the mask when we went down to the 1ˢᵗ floor for radiation…….next she posted them on face book…..what a culture we live in.

The prayers were answered my chemo **needle stick-"IV"** was not that bad at all, and they took blood at the same time. They took blood to establish a base line for my Red blood cells, white blood cells, and platelettes. The white blood cells to establish if the kidneys are at a safe level to continue treatment at the current dosage levels. After they took the blood and the IV was set-up in my right arm, I begin to look around and Michele was in an uncomfortable hospital chair, I had a roommate sitting across from me....I did not like this, but she was very humble and pleasant. They staff members were so nice there they brought me a lunch and were bringing me apple and grape juice through-out the day. They did a tutorial at the end of the day, gave me an entire notebook made up from cancer survivors who said this is want the people want to know.......reviewed the possible and most common side effects, nutrition and precautionary measures. I am taking a drug entitled "EMEND" and "Cisplatin"......both of which cause your hair to fall out.....what a bummer.....but it will grow back and my boss said I can wear a hat or any head covering of my choosing to any meetings whatsoever, due rag or baseball cap.

Tonight Michele and I will *"trim-up"* my crew cut....**if** my hair falls out, in 2-3 weeks we will know for certain.......10% loose hair on other parts of their body......hope is alive! Let me set the stage for you a little better here. As you well know...nobody stays in hospitals anymore they get you in and out quickly. So what do they do with all those rooms the hospitals originally built so many years ago? The hospital had taken the typical hospital rooms....... taken out all the beds in the wing, left the TV, put a doorway between the rooms and the nurses set up a portable station in the back of the rooms. So I constantly, had traffic in and out of the room where the nurses continually checked and replace the IV bags, and updated information in the portable computer system. I had to wait for the pharmacist to make up the chemical brew established by the doctor's orders based on my height and weight. Then they put in a bag to prep me with saline solution, then the finally after what seemed like about an hour wait the pharmacist came in with the bag, set it down..... the nurses reviewed the calculations.......then finally I started with the chemo medicine known as "Cisplatin", no burning, no coldness, no difference at all, the roommate left, and Michele started reading the bible 1st Samuel Chapters 26 through 2nd Samuel chapter 1.....wow the (8) attempts on David's life, and all the dark days he went through...... no wonder the psalms are so wonderful......David was "greatly inspired by the holy spirit of God as a writer". Anyway, as the day trudged onward after a little over an hour of this, and many *"urination-breaks"*

I finally finished this bag…..it was about 3:15 or so……so finally we started on the two IV bags that are supposed to "Flush-out-your-system" and then a nurse came and unhooked me where Michel and I went down to radiation, walked right in changed into my gown, sat down in the mini-waiting room, then we got board after 2 minutes and sat down at a puzzle table and tried to add some pieces to a puzzle in progress, but…… neither one of got a single piece and then I heard the voice of "Kreig " (radiation technician) saying Mr. Elliott there you are. Come on back, I signed the "Sign-in sheet with my picture on it (cool sheet) can't make any mistake about who you're treating this way………then they let Michele take a picture of me under the mask….of course these were posted on face book……then 9 minutes later (I timed them with my stop watch) they removed the mask and she took a picture with all the waffle marks on my face. Have I mentioned the mask is very, very, very tight………..it is!

Then I went into the room to speak with "Marlyin" the nutritionist who weighted me and warned me about losing weight and said she would be watching me. Then I stepped into a room to see the radiation doctor who was nowhere to be found. The nurse "Ann" gave me some mediated cream to put on the outside of my neck as time goes by. I exited the room dressed and Michele and I went back to Chemo Therapy where they hooked me up to the last of 4 IV bags and onward we went……. then Dr. "B" came to see me (the doctor that was nowhere to be found) and spoke with me about some prescription I had ask for, in the event I had a sore throat……said he would prescribe it to me, Dr. "B" has very good bedside manners, shook my hand said he would probably take a look at me on Tuesday, and every Monday they will have to draw blood and send it up to the chemo people to speed up the process. He shook my hand said he will probably look down my throat next week…….so I apparently see the doctor every "*Tuesday*" or every Chemo Day. (6) more times. After he left about 30 minutes went by another urinary break for me, and then "*Chrissie*" the nurse came and gave me a lecture on the chemo therapy, most common side effects, how the notebook is set up what to read (*all of it*), who wrote up what it consist of, and she stressed the point about my weight and how this is a key to recovery. At about 5:30 Michele and I left the hospital and boy was I tried, and she was too. Came home petted Kaya (Siberian Husky dog), walked the dog 2.4 miles…..checked out the pictures Michele posted to face book, feed the fish, cats, birds, (dog gets a bone), watched some TV as I napped/rested Michele made dinner, I called mother spoke with her/called sister spoke with her/called my cancer survivor deacon friend Ray, spoke with him / spoke with Sunday school friend Melissa /Michele called Bonnie(preacher wife and cancer survivor and a very good friend of Michele's'), I got to ask her a question about losing her hair…….I forgot to mentioned we stopped on the way home and I got a chocolate & vanilla milkshake………at "Whataburger"…….Finally, Michele and I ate dinner watched "Monk" and some other TV shows and crashed in the bed about 10:00 PM. I am writing this one day later than it actually transpired, and I can tell you……I feel **very tired**, and I have **lost my appetite** already, boy **this** is going to be a struggle.

2010_28_July Wednesday 3:30 PM (5 of 31 more radiation Treatment)   My first thought is only (31) more and I will be finished……yes!   Now here is what happened, I showed up walked in, signed in the log book at the counter, said hey to worker "Derrick" went to the next receptionist, gave them my name it was on the list the "volunteer worker" highlighted my name said go on back, I went into the official dressing rooms put my keys, sun glasses, watch into the locker, picked-up a gown, changed from the waist up……walked into the mini-waiting area took a seat. The radiation technicians check this area after every treatment, and after they check the appointment book….believe me they have not made me wait if I was out there alone. They called me in….I laid down on the table put my neck directly on the spot required…… they put a roll pillow under my legs for back support brought out this white mask (see face book for the picture) and away we go. The mask is clamped down very tight, and the machine makes a buzzing sound when they switch it on………after each treatment the technicians come out and make an adjustment, go back in the control booth and "zap" me again, come out tell me to raise my hand if I need anything go back into the control booth and after three "**Zap-pings**" I am "Unclamped" out of the very tight mask customized to fit my face only…..then the technician Kreig or Melanie grab my elbow and forearm to help me sit upright for a few seconds, I tell them good bye, exit out of the room, go down the hall and discard the gown in the "*dirty-gown bin*" put my shirt one, usually skip "*tucking-it-in*" and exit the building (this is the best part "*cancer-patients*" get to park right up front in a reserved parking lot) and I got in my car and headed for home. There I finally "said it" I am under the realization..........I am a **"Cancer Patient"** I remember when Grand Mother Burrell had cancer and I heard terms like "radiation & chemo therapy" and thought what in the world is that. How awful that must have been for Grandmother Burrell.......not to of had the technology we have, and the nausea medicines........was God preparing me then, I remember the week I was told she had cancer my 1st grade class had been doing a science study of cancer cells they gave us electron microscope pictures of the cancer cells and spoke about how fast they grow because these cell's duplicate rapidly.........I remember time was of the essence, when I learned that afternoon I had cancer I wanted to start the treatments that very day if possible time is of the essence........let's go doctor..........it's true I am very impatient but I am working on it. When your own mortality is at stake you want "*reprieve/liberation/help*" and you want if fast. It still rings in my head over and over again **"Cancer Patient"**.......will I be a victim or survivor...? Either way my walk with the Lord has been more intimate, and I am grateful. My thoughts are.......this could be a great testimony for me, and I could work on my "*sin of silence*" where I witness more often to anyone in my domain. I think.......going to the doctor on just a sore throat was that ever important.........my cancer was caught early. Ma-maw Burrell had she only gone to the OBGYN or female doctor every year, what if they had caught it early.....would she still be with us......or at least had a few more years.....only God knows, and God has his reasons. It was her time preordained before the earth began. Proverbs 3: 5-6 comes to mind   Trust in the LORD with all thine heart; and lean not unto thine own understanding. In all thy ways acknowledge him, and he shall direct thy paths. Executing this scripture is where the difficulty is in my own life, sure I can say it.....but living it out to the fullest extent is challenging, but the more I go to God in prayer and the more I am.......dare I say "longsuffering / patient......then I begin to be still and know my God will deliver me, not my way but God's way. I miss Ma-maw Burrell, and I have only been to her grave site one time on my own in my life. I can't help but wonder, how great that will be to see her in her "*new christlike body*" no cancer, not bad eye site, etc......will I recognize her at all, will some beautiful young lady 25 years old come up to me and say are you "Louise's son Dale" (me being 25 of course) and will she say you knew me as Ma-maw Burrell.......wow what a wonderful time. What will it be like, when after greeting our Lord and savior spending time with him, not desiring to leave him at all he is the reason I want to be in heaven, not rewards, not meeting the famous biblical heroes, but seeing my lord and savior who took the nails for me while I was yet a sinner, he will receive one of his blood bought children (who he had to spank a lot)......... Hopefully at some point he allows us to fellowship with our love ones who have gone before us oh how wonderful, the laughter. My thoughts today as I am coming to grips with the fact I am actually a "**Cancer Patient**".

2010_28_July Thursday 3:30 PM (6 of 30 more radiation Treatment)
My first thought is only (30) more and I will be finished......yes!
        Today the side affect of eh chemo is being very Nausea, and it woke me up in the middle of the night......took a general nausea pill about 4:30 this morning......have mercy...........back to the diary.......
Now here is what happened, I struggled through the day with bouts of nausea, and a belief it or not, I am so tired and no matter what I do I can't seem to get comfortable. I toss and turn in my chair at home; I can't seem to get comfortable when I take a nap neither. Even though I am tired thoughts keep racing through my head.

2010_29_July Friday 3:30 PM (6 of 29 more radiation Treatment)
My first thought is only (29) more and I will be finished......yes! I told the girls Brandi and Melanie my stethoscope joke.   T o d a y the side affect of eh chemo is being medium nausea, throughout the day. The wave of sickness passes but I can't seem to find comfort. As Friday night approaches, I find yet another side affect.....I am constipated, and uncomfortable, so Michele and I go talk to a pharmacist where I am getting my cancer drugs filled....CVS pharmacy......and this guy from India tells me to take one or two of these stool softener pills, actually picked them out from the shelf for me. I took one and had great hopes, I could not sleep comfortable, but I felt like I had to go and could not go......waiting and finally at 3:30 AM on Saturday morning I drove to work, I had forgotten to take two of my study materials home with me

and I went back at 3:30 AM to collect them at the office. No one much on the road at this hour but I did pass a couple of cars here and there, then when I got to the building I walked inside and ....wamo.....a bowel movement, yes I was happy, and finally some relief. I guess this sounds crazy when I write about it....but it's just the night before....... and all that misery. Then I felt good and I gathered my study materials shut down my computer system and headed home, I had drink so much water, I was in a *"tinkle-mode"* about every 30 minutes. When I got home, I did get some rest, but it was laced with 30 minute breaks, and I was generally miserable, and that is pretty much how the weekend shaped up after a 4 hour nap I was able to study my Sunday School Lesson, and then I was able to write some notes about it.

2010_01_August Sunday   Went to Sunday school and church, boy I was tired, and did not sleep good at all Saturday night. I was actually very exhausted and I barely made it through teaching Sunday school, only with Michele's help. The lesson was good, and the room was packed, but I was feeling very tired, and a little more anxious and apprehensive than normal. I had no patience but wanted to be there. Ray invited me and Michele over to his house for leftovers after a deer meat social he had the night before, but I was too uptight to totally relax and enjoy it. When we arrived home I tried to drink some fluids to counter act the drugs (chemo) but I was still miserable, and not looking forward to Monday morning.

2010_02_August Monday   I went to work today, Michele got up and made me some bacon cheese grits, but I have developed a new type of sore throat in my upper part of the back of my throat, hurts and does not seem to subside much with fluids. I am still drinking lots of fluids, I have to mail a letter to cousin Cindy, for some reason I forgot to send her thank-you note.........and I have to pick up two prescriptions today one is hopefully for a gargle and swallow throat mender, and one is for an "EMEND" pills for the 2nd chemo treatment. Today I have to get radiation, only 28 more, then I have to have blood drawn from my veins, and sent up to the chemo people so the therapy goes faster tomorrow. I am off to morrow, and believe me.......If I had the time I could use about (6) weeks off right not but that is not an option. I have developed a rash on the right side of my neck that is bothering me now, it is irritated but I have put some lotion on it for some relief. At 8:00 AM I take my (2) stool softener pills and my general pill for nausea. This seems to help; this chemo is like putting poison in your system, the body is not made for this......! My thoughts are being obsessed with the health issues; I can't focus on much else other than the misery I am in. Wow here he go again week (2) has only just begun.......am I going to make it, I need God in my life right now so much......I am having trouble sleeping, my throat hurts, and I am not able to keep an optimistic outlook right now. It is only 08:10 AM what am I going to do........hold on tight and weather the storm, God be with me as I embark on this "daily".......:"Pre-adventure".

2010_03_August Tuesday   I did not go to work today........Michele got up and made me some bacon chopped it in cheese grits (excellent). Even though she does not eat cheese grits, she sure can make them good. We arrived at 10:30 and got up on the third floor where we had about a 45 minute wait. I had gained a pound or two and this is good in the doctor's eyes. Once I showed them my old sun-poison type of rash that had *"flared-up"* this turned out to be a very good thing. They put me in a private room (YES)! They wanted to make sure it was not contagious, and they started the IV about 11:45 AM with a big bag of saline solution. The......."*stick/sting*".......was not bad at all (thank-you) many answered prayers......I hate this part getting stuck in the arm..........my labs were done and we started rolling along. Michele went downstairs to get some lunch a burger and curly fries and a chocolate chip cookie a 10 inch one......we would later share. Then the staff "Samantha" brought me a sealed sandwich lunch with tomatoes and orange a ham sandwich and a bag of chips..........delicious. I put some mustard on my ham sandwich and it went down better, the orange.......Michele peeled for me and I ate it all it.......tasted so good. Then Michele read in the bible to me for about 3-4 chapters until she got very sleepy as did I ....so you know what we did.......we took a nap for about an hour. The hours dragged on as I got up and down trying to make the most of my day then about 2:30 they started the chemo therapy "cystapltin" drug and away we went. Another long and laborious hour.......while this was going on Julie (co-worker) and her Husband Dan were fasting for me and she sent me the sweetest email: May you see that there are just one pair of footprints in the sand through this journey and know always that you are being carried through the valley. We are with you too, standing firm for all that God has for you and that this would align to your hopes and prayers. Praying these versus over you today. Praying for his strength to be made perfect in your weakness and that any fear would be casted aside and that it would be filled 10 fold with His most perfect love for you and your love for Him.2 Corinthians 12:9 (King James Version): 9And he said unto me, My grace is sufficient for thee: for my strength is made perfect in weakness. Most gladly therefore will I rather glory in my infirmities, that the power of Christ may rest upon me.1 John 4:18 (King James Version): There is no fear in love; but perfect love casteth out fear: because fear hath torment. He that feareth is not made perfect in love. This was received on day later but it meant a lot to me. I received a letter/card from my sister and mother both equally as precious. And Melissa in Lithia Springs sent me an email saying I have been praying for you. How thoughtful and appreciated........from a grateful heart. I pray I am not loosing site of the lesson and thing(s) God is teaching me, and I look forward to establishing a new and wonderful testimony, if this is the outcome In God's plans for me. On the next page I want to address the side effects.

I am suffering from the following side affects

I am feeling the following side affects trying to offset them with prayers and medications:

1. Unnaturally tired --- trying to pump iron & lots of prayers to combat this
2. Nausea --- taking pills & lost of prayers to combat this
3. Lack of sleep --- taking Benadryl at night & lots of prayers to combat this
4. Sporadic hiccups --- only one about every 4-6 hours strange but true
5. Constipation --- Stool softeners (3) at 8AM & lost of prayers to combat this
6. Sore throat in the upper back side --- gargling special medicine and swallowing 1st thing in the morning and last thing at night.

7. Mentally preparing to start losing all of my hair on top of my head --- purchased a Christina toboggan type cap with a cross on it and it says "MY Redeemer" on the other side of it. Orange and Black.

8. Will be shopping at Wall Mart to get some "FSU" or "Gator" crocks to start wearing to the hospital during those **long** chemo days.

9. Taking a special pill and putting lotion on my skin where a rash developed near the radiation area.

10. Mentally --- reading scripture writing in my diary & lots of prayers to combat this.

Outside of the aforementioned side effects.....I am doing ok. I keep thinking about the fear of the unknown and how that plays on our mind, but then I think about being a mature Christian and having the attitude Michele has reminded me so often of.........I can't wait to see what God has in store for me next. Brother this takes great faith..........let me tell you. If I am to grow in grace and knowledge as the holy scripture say in 2nd Peter 3: 18............then first I have to learn this 1 John 4:18 (King James Version)**:** There is **no** fear in love; but perfect love casteth out fear: because fear hath torment. He that feareth is not made perfect in love. That is a tough one to learn, I remember Grandmother Elliott teaching me as a 4 year old, Psalms 56:3 "What time I am afraid I will trust in thee", ...boy is this ever true. Sometimes the fear is of the unknown, sometimes it's a financial fear, sometimes it is a provider fear, etc.......but learning to walk and grow and trust God is so important. After the bag of chemo finished Michele and I took a break and went downstairs to take radiation wow that was a trip fast and furious, we spoke with the nutritionist and she was happy I had gained a pound or two, then we spoke with the doctor and he examined the rash on my neck, agreed with the other physicians prescription and said if it does not work we will have a determalogist take a look at it but the medication should work. After that we made it back up to chemo where they essentially unhooked the bag and it was about 4:30 PM Michele and I went down one floor to visits a church member Brian Morris and he had just had is entire prostrate removed and he was now in recovery we prayed, laugh, visited and then left. We went to "Lifeway" store where I purchased a special cap for **when**

I go bald; it says "redeemer" on one side has a cross on the other side. I got another triquetra necklace (black) and a cross that says "Cosmic Truth" on the backside of it. Here is what most dictionaries say about COSMIC TRUTH - *1 a : of or relating to the cosmos, the extraterrestrial vastness, or the universe in contrast to the earth alone b : of, relating to, or concerned with abstract spiritual or metaphysical ideas 2 : characterized by greatness especially in extent, intensity, or comprehensiveness <a cosmic thinker> <cosmic truth>*

I have noticed my throat hurts a little in the upper back portion, I tried drinking a cold smoothie, but that did no help much. Anyway the "cosmic truth" was nailed to the cross for us, by us, under the authority of God therefore being the only true....... *"Cosmic Truth"*

2010_03_August Wednesday   Only 25 more trips to radiation, and I will be through….yes……..nothing eventful just 10 minutes in on the table and right out. On the way home I got in the worst thunderstorm ever. I made it home before dark and it was clear at the house.

2010_04_August Thursday   Only 24 more trips to radiation, and I will be through….yes……..nothing eventful just 10 minutes in on the table and right out. I got home and found the energy to cut the grass "front yard only" then I took a shower, walked Kaya (dog) and ate very little with Michele, took my medicine(s), the rash on my back and shoulder have made tremendous progress and are clearing up just great. I took a nap and then my Benadryl and went to bed at 8:34 PM. Slept good mother and Aunt Hazel made it home safe from Braselton GA, apparently Aunt Hazel had to have two teeth pulled near there and they stopped by Sandy's house to eat and wait out the traffic a little.

2010_05_August Friday   Only 23 more trips to radiation, and I will be through….yes……..nothing eventful just 10 minutes in on the table and right out. I got home and found no energy for much of anything. I almost rode the motorcycle but the weather report called for 30 % chance of isolated thunderstorms. This is right on the margin of my *"GO or NOGO"* decision threshold. Seeing how I do not like lingering in the afternoon and I was not driving straight home I decided not to ride the motorcycle, and what a good decision that was. "NO-GO" was the right decision. Missed the Men's Friday Morning Breakfast, but I just did not feel like going. After I got home on Thursday evening I had all the energy zapped out of me. I was so exhausted that on Friday morning I had to leave the office at 10:00 AM and go home for the day. I slept until about 4:00 and then I had to force myself to stay-up. I did not like the weekend I was tired and nausea, and my throat hurt, and I did not feel good. I did have an appetite for honey nut cereal, and whole D milk. So on Saturday morning I got up rode the motorcycle and got some milk and cereal and two fresh tomatoes. I had honey nut cheerios for breakfast and guess what the food has lost a lot of its taste. Then for lunch I was so excited and I had two tomatoes sandwiches with cheese and mayonnaise, but the food is losing its <u>taste</u> for me. Saturday I got some much needed rest. I am telling the you.............. the number one side affect is that dang "chemo-therapy" makes you feel so "***very tired***".........you are out of energy. I still managed to get up and run the "weed-eater" around the entire inside of the fence and fix the spot where the deer had clambered over it in the back side corner. Electric fence is working again, Kaya never knew it was off, but it was shorted out for a while. I felt miserable Saturday for the most part, even after a shower and a nap, nothing put me in a better mood, even show shopping left its damper effect, I could not find any crocks or good sandals to buy. Sunday I went to church and my spirit was lifted up somewhat, even though I could not concentrate much and did not get to teach.........I still received a blessing by getting to hear our youth program and we went out to eat with some church family members, then Michele became emotionally teary eyed when she recanted my cancer story to some of our church family members, it really is hard on her, not being able to help much, just waiting in the wings.

2010_09_August Monday   This can't be right, only 23 more trips to radiation, and I will be through....I guess I was one off the mark on Friday......yes.......These Mondays have become to be known as "**Bloody Mondays'** " due to the fact I have to get my blood drawn from the nurse Jessica, hopefully, I set this up with her last time, she comes down ties up my arm, I put on my blindfold and she says little stick and in a couple of minutes it's all over with and my medications are on their way up to the *"chemo-people"* and hopefully all will go well and I will have nothing eventful just 10 minutes in on the table and right out. I got home and found out I need to actually cut the back yard aka south 40 this week, not sure when that's going to happen. The *"chemo-people"* are super nice and wonderful individuals, it's just that I personally hate having that *"poison"* aka medicine in my system. I am supposed to lose my hair this week my head feels dryer than usual, and I am really apprehensive about this I know it will grow back in time and it's just a brief season, but still I.......like all those who have gone before me am very apprehensive and uptight about this.............maybe it will come back solid white. Ok so I am over it already, I will keep you posted on how I am feeling. God is Good........all the time!

2010_10_August Tuesday   Only (4) more days of chemo therapy, come on Dale you can survive this just think........this is a lot better than three weeks ago. Go Dale Go.......push.......go forth........ sojourn! I am still not happy about this......but let the adventure begin another long and dreadful day with the *"chemo-people"* doing their job as pleasantly and joyfully as possible......meanwhile back at camp Dale misery, doom gloom, waiting to be pricked, and zapped like a bug under a weird human experiment in the radiation room, and atop it all you don't have to pull your hair out.............it will fall out on it's on....... serenity now!!!!!

I was humbled when I spoke to the bishop's wife this weekend. Her name is Bonnie and she not only had to have a "port" (surgery IV in skin) but she had to have six (6) months not weeks but months of *"chemo-people"* aka therapy..........so there count yourself very very fortunate at least you don't have to have a port and **6-months** of chemo therapy aka chemo -people. Michele and I arrived there at 10:00 and I was a little irritated because **they** had fumbled the orders and did not draw my blood on Monday (as usual) because they did not have doctor's orders. But for whatever reason the entire process went smooth, I was sharing a room with a lady who slept then entire time. Michele and I got there settled down and a nurse named "Christina" came and did the dreaded........"Stick/Prick" in the arm IV prep work. It was not all that bad, (answered prayers) then they started the big bag of saline solution, Michele set up shop there emptying out all the "snacks" she brought *"cheese-it gold fish"*, *animal crackers, peanut butter crackers, and a bottle of trail mix.* I sat there an hour and they brought lunch in and away we went into making me a ham sandwich with mustard and tomato, baked lays potato chips, and Michele hand peeled my orange........one bad side affect in full force now is my taste buds are being killed off, and trust me meats do not taste good to me, and most of the foods are beginning to taste very very very bland like mush. Some people have described them as tasting like metals or saw dust, I have never ate saw dust, or metals........but I understand **what** they are saying vey very tasteless, and all foods taste the same really.

After I ate Michele read the bible to me for quite a while 2nd Samuel where David was extending an act of kindness to Jonathan son misphhobosheth (King Saul's grandson). Then we actually finished the chemo "citsplatin" aka poison........an hour later so at 3:30 we were totally finished and ready to go to radiation. Yes the day went smooth, and after radiation, I spoke with the nutrientist who told me to avoid extreme *"hots and colds"* but said I would be perfectly ok to try *"spicy"* foods seeing how my taste buds were being killed off.....back to jalapeño (*love them*). Then I went in to see Doctor"B", and he stuck that camera with the spaghetti hose on the end of it down my nose and through to my throat and back of my tongue (*of course Michele filmed this it's on face book*) and then he delivered the good news........Mr. Elliott that tumor that was on the back of your tongue that I said was reduced by 70% last week has completely disappeared. God is Good, All the time. AMEN!!!!!

This was great news listen up carefully here, when Dr. "G" first examined me he saw the same tumor using the *"camera/scope"* that Dr. "B" saw and this is the tumor they are talking about. Caveat here is after my (3) hour biopsy, Dr. "G" found a small tumor aka 2nd tumor the size of a small pea next to my *"carotid artery"* and he definitely identified this pea size tumor as the source of my cancer. So on this tumor I have no news, but in a *follow-up* appointment Dr. "G" said he would definitely do a cleanup surgery.......Not sure how intense this will be, but it will be 4-6 weeks after chemo & radiation are over with an ending date for chemo & radiation is somewhere around September 10, 2010. During the day the Chemo doctor Dr."BRO" aka Learch aka Giant aka big man, came to see me and said I was not going to lose my hair......

so happy……..and said I am doing good…….no need for labs (blood drawn) next week. Michele and I are doing well and we actually got home at about 5:30 so it was a good day for me and I went outside got on the riding lawnmower and cut then entire back yard, showered, and shaved and sat in front of the TV by 7:30 unbelievable…what a good day. God is good all the time AMEN!

2010_11_August Wednesday   Only (20) more days of radiation, come on Dale you can survive and tonight is Wednesday   church I went to radiation treatment, then I went to the gift shop nothing there, went to deposit 16:50 check in our bank (we have a dispute of bank fees right now) Michele is looking into this. I fell better than usual and not nearly as sick and I have in the past two weeks. I felts so good, when I got home I received some instructions from Michele & went out to the Wall Mart Superstore in Crawfordville, made a deposit in envision (our bank) purchase (4) pair of brown jeans and some ankle boots, and a gator hat. Kaya did not make the trip with me. It rained cats and dogs on the way home. Our sprinklers system is not working for some reason. The breaker is not off set , the switch is on, and the timer appears to be working, this is a mystery. Anyway not really bouts of nausea today, so I am in a really good mood. I am not sure why but we missed church tonight.

2010_12_August Thursday   only (19) more days of radiation, come on Dale you can survive and tonight is known as "WGCN" that stands for "weekly grass cutting night". Why on Thursdays you might ask, well that gives you a (2) day rain delay in case of inclement weather conditions……..here in this neck of the woods it rains 3-5 times a week during the summer time. Any way I went to radiation treatment, 10 minutes in and out, new side affect is I don't have to shave my neck anymore. I still do out of habit. I am going to see my primary care physician about my "neck/upper shoulder rash". I have only one more pill and then I am out of medicine for this. I have an appointment tomorrow at 11:00 with Dr. "W" (primary care) to see if he can refer me to a dermatologist. I want to have a couple of moles removed as well.

2010_13_August Friday   only (18) more days of radiation, come on Dale you can survive. I saw Dr. "W" my primary care physician today and he referred me to a dermatologist. So I have an appointment at 11:00 on Monday to talk with the dermatologist about the skin rash. Friday I was not feeling too good for some reason and I have **no taste buds** thus making it very difficult to eat anything. All foods especially meats taste terrible, but I am forcing myself to eat it anyway. The ever posing threat of a feeding tube does not sound too appealing to me. Fruits are my friends.......and Michele and I are thinking about getting a blender and definitely getting some yogurts and softer foods. At least 6 more weeks of eating food with no taste, how will I survive this, I don't know but it's definitely not going to be easy, who would have thought that something as simple as eating would become some out right "**tasks**" or a very unpleasant thing to do........certainly not me, I had not forgotten how much *fun* eating and enjoying a good tasting meal was. But when this is taken away from you.......you realize how much that means to you.....no taste buds wow now that's a recipe for a diet if ever there was one. My throat is a little sore not too bad, but it really hurts to yawn. I try to avoid this and for some strange reason the side affect of hiccups occurs more often............so I hold my breath to stop the hiccups this is the only thing that really works for me. The main side effect for me now is the killing of my taste buds. Eating is not so easy anymore.

2010_16_August Monday   only (17) more days of radiation, come on Dale you can survive. I called the dermatologist and made an appointment for 11:00 today. So let's see how this goes. It went well this weight lifter looking guy came into the room (doctor's office) and introduced himself as Dr. "WA" and he ask me to take off my shirt examined me and then said I am not sure that is "*fungal*" on your neck, so he sliced off sever samples with a scalpel, *not too painful*, put them on a microscope slide and said Mr. Elliott I will be right back. He sent another doctor in the room, for observation, then he left and eventually the weight lifter doctor came back into the room with a massive camera around his neck, and he took several picture of my condition on my neck.........and said that is fungal, so I have written a prescription it's at south wood, and you can have these samples the nurse will give you for a cream. He said I will see you in two weeks……..and keep taking the medicine I prescribe until the bottle is empty. He left the room, and I got my shirt on and left. Not bad at all I stopped at McDonald's and got a big Mack meal, called Michele educated her on the status of the dermatologist appointment and struggled to get down a "big-Mack"…. no fries…….then I went back to work. My buddy Mark made my day today……he gave me some rain gear for motorcycle riding…….coat & pants……….Yes a good day so far.

2010_17_August Tuesday   only (16) more days of radiation, Only (3) more Chemo-Therapy sessions………come on Dale you can survive. Michele and I arrived at 09:30 where I got radiation treatment 1st thing………boy do I have a well developed ring of what looks like a sun burn around my neck. I have some Vitim A, B, C, & D lotion to put on it. It does not burn like a sun burn or even fell hot like sunburn does on the skin. But it looks like…"(tanish-redish like)" sunburn. After the 10 minutes on the radiation table….zap, zap, zap……..(They administered radiation in three places) we went up to the third floor and started the long and laborious day on the chemo therapy treatment. This is how it works….this is what happens……we get there at 09:45 and sign-in on a log book and I say hey to a girl named Samantha. We have a "sit and wait period" for the nursing staff to get the doctor's orders together and decide where my pharmaceuticals orders are, so they can physically give them (each week) to the on duty pharmacist who fills the biohazard material prescription for the……2 pints of starter saline solution (1st two hours), followed by 1-pint of "citsplatin" ,(1 hour) of this poison aka medicine, followed by 1 pint of something that preserves my kidneys, not sure what this is (1-hour bag) of it…..followed by about 4-5 more ounces of saline solution. Before this begins we *"sit & wait"* for about an hour each time we go….then they weigh me, take my blood pressure, temperature, monitor my heart rate during the temp & blood pressure check, then put on a hospital bracelet with my name, date-of-birth, age, male, & serial numbers aka Id numbers the nursing staff references before administering the medications. So we arrive wait an hour then they finally take me back to a semi-private room where I sit in a uncomfortable hospital recliner from about "***10:30 AM -3:30 PM***". Bonnie and her son Tyler came to visit me today and they brought me cookies.......yes!!!!............ Once in the recliner, a nurse comes with plastic gloves and a kit of stuff wrapped in plastic and says ok we need to start your IV, she opens the kit, wraps a rubber tourniquet around my upper bicep muscle and starts slapping the vein area where I am going to get *"stuck/pricked"* with the IV needle. After about a minute of this she swabs some cotton on my arm, and then some alcohol and I look away and like my sister Sandy told me try to focus on something else in your mind "totally"......I hear the nurse say ok 1, 2, 3 stick......"**pain**" of the needle going into the vein......then once the nurse gives me the "**bee sting**" as I call it the pain subsides, and she tapes it down tight, and then she grabs a syringe and test the stick to make sure she is actually in a vein and can pull blood out and push fluid in, then she hooks up the Saline solution and this drip starts it takes a little over (2) hours and they let about 4-5 oz stay in the bottom of the bag for a final flush later. Then about "1 ½" hours into this a lady volunteer come by and ask if I would like a lunch........today I said yes because it was chicken salad, but truthfully it tasted like cardboard......then when about two hours have transpired I get to start the actually chemotherapy of the drug "citsplatin", the nurse puts on rubber gloves and a special water proof gown, and opens the bag and starts the IV........it takes the pint back a little over an hour to drip through, and then when this finishes they start the bag of "*kidney saver*" flush this takes a little over an hour, then after this they switch lines and the IV switches over flushing the last of the 4-5 ounces saline solution. After this I usually go down stairs get 10 minutes of radiation (except for today only) and then I speak with a person who has their PHD in nutrition......they weigh me, and advise me on eating habits, making some suggestions her e and there, then I "*sit & wait*" to see the radiation doctor who advises me on the progress or my radiation therapy and what to expect next. Then by this time it's about 4:30 so Michele and I go home. On the way home I call My mom and give her a status, and if I can get in touch with my sister Sandy I call her too. I felt so very tired last night I went to bed at 9:30 PM.

2010_18_August Wednesday   only (15) more days of radiation, come on Dale you can survive. I am an old pro at this now......I drive to the gate pick up the phone call them say "Dale Elliott here for my radiation appointment"......they open the gate, and I park in the "VIP gated parking lot" for cancer patients only. I walk in through two glass doors, sign in the log book, say hey to the receptionist and tell them my name and "*sit & wait*" usually not long.......then the radiation people call the receptionist and send me back where I change into a gown from the waist up, go to another "sit & wait" mini-waiting area where usually very quickly sometimes I don't even sit down and they call me back. I sign-on the log book and put my initials and date the number of treatments like 18 of 35 etc.........then the wonderful staff members who are very friendly........strap me down in the tight tight tight mask. Zap me three times (10 minutes) I put my glasses back on rub my face and forehead to smoother the tightness away, I go back to the dressing room put my shirt back on.......and I am out of there said bye to the worker "Derrick" and "Telishia" walked through the double foyer doors cross the drive way and I am in my car headed home sweet home.

2010_19_August Thursday   only (14) more days of radiation, I am tired and weary today at work it is only 2:03 PM in the afternoon but I am worn out and ready for a nap. My neck is sore, my lymph node seems to be going down and not nearly as swollen as it has been in the past. My throat is sore but the biggest and worst problem I am having is I can't taste anything and it's getting worse every day, life is not the same just not being able to taste food.

2010_23_AugustMonday   only (13) more days of radiation, come on Dale you can survive. Radiation went off without a hitch same ole song and dance 10 minutes on the table in & out just fine, felt terribly tired but went home and took a nap. Got up at 6:30 went outside and spent one hour cutting the backyard on the riding lawnmower.

2010_24_August Tuesday   only (3) more treatments of "Chemo-Therapy" counting today.....I am struggling, but I think I am going to make it.........Michele and I arrived at 10:00 and I was in radiation for about 40 minutes they had to narrow down the area they are going to start treating....they have been treating 3 general areas of my neck, now they will start treating 4 specific areas of my neck, much narrower than in the past few weeks. I was exceedingly glad........ to get out of that mask today. Then Michele and I went upstairs to chemo-therapy......having arrived so late 11:00 I thought wow this is going to take some time......as it turned out it went well, and I have lost about 10lbs. but my blood pressure and vital signs were robust. They took us in right away and we got a private room.........I was then.......stuck/pricked/ IV installed........bob that hurt this time....... taped down and taped up......they have this new tape that does not stick to your hair on the arms.......very grateful and thankful for that invention...........Michele went downstairs and got me some "broccoli cheese soup" a large bowl from the hospital cafeteria......I was able to eat all of it......boy was it good. Stephanie works close by and she came up to see Michele and I during her lunch hour........Stephanie is such a wonderful person we laughed and had a really good visit. She left and the laborious "IV dripping" continued.....Michele had prepared snacks for me as she always does but I could not eat much it hurts my throat to swallow and to eat anything other than soft foods. Yesterday Stephanie purchased me a "Big Mack" from McDonalds.....I wanted it so bad but I could only manage to literally choke down ½ of it at best.....it was rough without any taste buds all food is really a struggle to get down my throat. It either burns or taste so bad......like I am literally chewing rubber, paper, or cardboard............ I can't seem to eat it. It is so hard to understand this unless you have gone through this and actually lost your taste buds......otherwise you don't really get it. I came across something similar when I hurt my back and could not walk from lifting something too heavy........pain like I had never experienced before and I literally could not focus on anything other than my back and had to take time off from work.........unless you have suffer through this you don't know what somebody is actually taking about......for me I used to think boy these old people "belly-ache" a lot about nothing......until it *actually happened to me*.....then wow......was that a horse of a different color.........the pain was almost more than I could bear. Same here with the taste buds being killed off due to chemo-therapy........some people thing great just eat foods you don't like what do you care.....you can't taste it anyway...........but I tell you the food itself if somewhat repulsive to you.....you are not actually in the mood to eat.......the desire to eat goes away, along with your appetite. Eating becomes a task, choir, and work.....anything but pleasure. Normally eating with taste buds is pleasurable, but not so once chemo-therapy kills off the taste buds.........I fight back the burning urge to walk down the halls of.........chemo-therapy.........cleanly painted walls........and take a can of spray paint and write *"eating sucks"* thanks to chemo-therapy.......hahahahhahaha......I would never do that.....but everybody undergoing chemo-therapy would pass that and say "AMEN".......but negative message are never good. God will help me through this.......I had Michele stop by Winn-Dixie....we purchased some soups.........and yes.....I was able to get it down last night. Michele read the bible to me yesterday about David's sons.... on raping his sister and the other one killing him for doing this about a year later. Then Absalom ran from David and he did not see his son for three years. Then I took a nap while listening to my Ipod..... Michele took a nap too.........We left at about 4:20 PM.......man was I glad to get home.....still took a nap boy was I tired...............got up and watch some TV ate some soup...........watched an episode of Monk..............

2010_25_August Wednesday   only (11) more days of radiation, come on Dale you can survive. I have a card for Dreama and Missy the "chemo-therapy" staff..........by the way the chemo-staff member have been wonderful and get the highest reviews from me. It's the poison aka medicine in my system I don't like, sometimes my fingers get number and tingly and sometimes I am a little dizzy, but this is normal and does not last for long..........ah but the worst side effect is......... killing the taste buds......2nd would be losing the hair.........but I have been fortunate so far I have not lost any hair.....knock on wood......... Dr. "BRO" said I **should not** lose my hair......so hopefully 60mg of citsplatin will not cause me to lose the hair. How do I feel.....waves of nausea..........consistently tired and sickish.

2010_26_August Thursday   only (10) more days of radiation, come on Dale you can survive. I was feeling so bad yesterday I left at 12:00.......struggling with bouts of nausea and I seem to have no desire to eat anything........I have no cravings nor any appetite. I was in radiation for a while they made some other adjustments and I am just not feeling well. My neck is like a bad sunburn and I am putting lotion on it but the sunburn effect is taking place it has begin to itch a little

and I am warm just like a sunburn. Generally I am very very tired.......
they tell me this late in the stage of radiation and chemo-therapy this is
normal......I can't stress how true this is I feel like sleeping and that's
about it.

2010_27_August Friday   only (09) more days of radiation,
come on Dale you can survive, your down to single digits. I have a
doctor's appointment with Dr. "G", I will ask him to schedule surgery
on Tuesday November 2nd for the *"clean-up "* surgery that will be 7
weeks after my last radiation & chemo-therapy........radiation today
at 2:45.......more fine tuning adjustments........then travel around the
building and see Dr. "G" on the 5th floor. Let's see what he has to
say......worst weekend of my life it hurts to swallow, and I can only
eat soft, soft, foods like soup or jello.......even bananas and milk hurt
to swallow.....I am burnt to a crisp on the outside of my throat like a
bad sunburn......I am going to ask Dr. "B".......If this week can be my
last week of radiation.....I don't think I can return for another three
days next week of being zapped in radiation......I will try and talk to
Dr. "BRO" on Tuesday about it being my last day of chemo-therapy
too......they are killing me the poison.......I can't handle it anymore.

2010_30_August Monday   only (08) more days of radiation,
come on Dale you can survive, I am feeling very tired, and even after I
rest with a nap......I get up and it's like I never did "recharge" I am still
very tired. My ears are even getting sunburned on the bottom. I had
the most miserable weekend Friday night I went home and took a nap
and watched some TV felt terrible, more of the same on Saturday, and
Sunday I could not even go to church.........I tell you I am in a state of
misery. Sore throat, I gag a lot , feel nausea, and generally feel too tired
to do anything. I am going to ask Dr. "BRO" if I can have this last one
as my final chemo-therapy treatment.......?

2010_30_August Tuesday   only (2) more treatments of
chemo-therapy, come on Dale you can survive. Michele and I arrived
at about 10:00 and went upstairs to the third floor, they took my vital
signs all ok.....weighed me 155.....only lost 4 lbs. They had ask me to
come upstairs yesterday at 3:45 to do my labs......but Ignore them.....

why be stuck/pricked today and tomorrow when I could just have the labs done at the same time I am being stuck for the IV aka chemo therapy. When I was walking down the hallway to my room the nurse "John" said to me there was some fumble yesterday on the labs but I can quickly do them today.....I just smiled. I tried to start having this done every Monday like they "chemo people" told me too, but they said after week 2 we can draw for labs unless we have the doctors orders so the orders always lagged a little but I guess they came early after about 6 weeks of lagging. Anyway Michele and I dropped off my car to have the oil changed at Mighty Muffler with Melvin , who spoke to me and said he would pray for me that some of the pain would be lifted off me.....it worked the stick/prick was almost painless this time and went off without any problems. Dr. "BRO" the chemo therapist doctor came in to see me at about 11:00 AM. I explained to him this had been the roughest week of my life, last week and even drinking water was gagging me some times, and I felt like my body was being pushed to the edge of the envelope, I only had three days of radiation next week and I ask him if this could be the last treatment of chemo-therapy and he assured me for medical reason this indeed could be the last treatment. I was so excited to hear this news.......I am telling you the chemo is killing me.........bad news is it can take 4 weeks to 4 months for my taste buds to return. Just hearing that made me feel better. I finally put on a gown because my shirt was rubbing against my neck and the sun burn part of the radiation was slightly irritating me. A girl from FSM's music department came by and played the guitar and sang some songs for me it was so nice. She left after I started talking to Dr. "BRO" and Michele and I had some lunch, and Michele drew up some sketches of how the judgment house scene was going to look. We finished on time 3:30 and it was off to radiation, where I was zapped like a bug, and it seem like they took longer than usual. Dr. "B" saw me and said there is no way you can finish up by Friday you need the last three days of radiation. So I will attend the last three days but under protest.......I am literally burnt from the inside out.

2010_01_September Wednesday   only (06) more days of radiation, come on Dale you can survive, They have changed the area to zap aka radiate a much smaller area.....takes a little longer but it is not burning my entire neck........in and out in about 15 minutes. Yesterday I took a new drug for being nausea and it caused me to be so drowsy I went to sleepy at 7:00 until the morning hours.

2010_02_September Thursday   only (05) more days of radiation, come on Dale you can survive,. Appointment at 10:00 today. Feeling very nausea from the chemo-therapy . I had a hard time with milk and cereal today. Took the emend "anti-nausea" pills at 9:30 instead of 11:45.......Not feeling well today not sure how I am going to hang in here at work. Fixing to leave and go to the 10:00 radiation session scheduled for today. Came back to work and felt so very tired, but held in there until 3:00 PM quitting time, went home and took a nap. Michele and I started doing a puzzle on the table amazing how the captures your attention. Felt very nausea and barley ate some broccoli cheese soup. I can't stress how bad food taste in general to me right now. I pray for a quick recovery of my taste buds.

2010_03_September Friday   only (04) more days of radiation, come on Dale you can survive. The area of my treatments is much smaller and the sun burn had been clearing up somewhat, of course I am putting lotion A,B,C,& D they gave me at the cancer unit for my neck and it seems to be healing up pretty good. Boy, am I glad today is Friday and I am off Monday for Labor Day. I ate some cheese grits and bacon this morning Michele fixed for me......could not taste it, but I know I have to eat to be healthy and this is very difficult for me right now.

2010_06_September Monday   Closed for the Labor Day holiday. No treatments.

2010_07_September Tuesday only (03) more days of radiation, come on Dale you can survive. I have felt bad over the long holiday weekend, so bad that I had to work from home on Tuesday. This was one of the worst weekends of my life the Nausea feeling, and unable to eat much at all.

2010_08_September Wednesday   only (02) more days of radiation, come on Dale you can survive. Today at work I was feeling a little better, but not much. It hurts to talk and swallow now. The radiation has totally killed my taste buds and it may be 3-4- months before they return. I am praying and hoping for a much sooner results so I can regain my health.

2010_09_September Thursday   Last day or radiation congratulations Dale you made it through 35 treatments of radiation and 6 weeks of chemo-therapy…….Dale….. Now I am on the road to recover. The good people at the Cancer Center gave me a certificate of completion (I am framing)…..I was also given my mask……..which pushed me to the limits of begin somewhat claustrophobic……..I have earned it and with great respect I walked out of the cancer center today hopefully to never return. My body has been pushed to the limits and I have endured a long road of treatments. Today I feel……. oh so ever nausea and just feel run down and tired. My throat is sore, and I can't swallow to easy. I fear I will lose more weight soon, not by choice, but because of circumstances. The battle has been difficult and no one understands…….if you can't taste it just eat it………the part they don't get is the food or liquid is repulsive to me. Until you have you taste buds taken away from you….. this makes very little sense…….. I am struggling I tell you I am struggling. Dark days I tell you…….!!!

2010_07_October Thursday   I had radical neck dissection surgery today, and my mother Louise, and sister Sandy came down to Tallahassee Florida to be with me. Surgery went fine and I was moved to a room, where I was assigned after the anesthesia wore off. Michele, Mom, and Sandy were there in the room. My dad was not feeling well enough to make the trip, but he was praying for me at home. How wonderful it is to be blessed with parents who believe in Jesus. I had some anesthesia sickness and almost hurled after I sat down from standing up to tinkle. Wow this was no fun, and I discovered I had 13 staple stitches on the outside of my neck, it really looked like a zipper, and I had 14 dissolvable stitches on the inside of my neck. I had this whole in the side of my neck where a drainage tube was coming out, and it empty into a little vile, pinned to my hospital gown. It was not too uncomfortable, the biggest part was the numbness down the right side of my neck, and the shock of when I looked in the mirror and saw the eight inches of zipper like staples......it freaked me out a little.

2010_08_October Friday   I got to go home today at 5:00 PM, I get the drainage tube out on Monday, (can't wait) and the staples out in about on the 21st of October. No real pain, at all this surgery went very smooth and other than the zipper I feel tired but good.

2010_09_October Saturday   I have notice the taste bud are not coming back in full force like they were. Michele went to Church today at 8:00 AM to help on the construction of Judgment House. Mom, Sandy, and I went to CVS pharmacy, and at lunch at a buffet in Wakulla County where they serve fried chicken, mash potatoes, green beans, corn bread, and sweet tea. Mom and Sandy will leave in the morning and Go home (State of Georgia).

2010_11_October Monday   I got the drainage tube out....... wow am I glad to get rid of that vile and drainage tube. It did not hurt, but it was slightly uncomfortable.

2010_21_October Monday   I Got the staple stitches out..... and this was actually pleasant, not painful at all. My scar is healing nicely. I feel so, much better. The soreness, and nausea have gone away, but the taste buds are not fully recovered yet.

It is now early November 2010.....This is how my summer went, I hope all who read this have had a much better and far more pleasant summer.

This was the most difficult summer of my life, but I have held the invisible hand of the Lord through it, and when my mind is fixed on the Lord, I find peace.

The End.

10. ABOUT THE AUTHOR

Dale was born in Atlanta Georgia, and lived there most of his adult life. He now currently resides on the outskirts of Tallahassee Florida in an urban area where life has a unique flavor and serene urban serenity (Wakulla County). Dale has one dog named Kaya she is a husky. Dale has three Scottish fold cats…..Abbie, Eddie, & Scottie……none of which are too crazy about Kaya. Dale has a Bachelor of Science in Geology, and a Bachelor of Arts in Accounting. Since Dale has been going through cancer, life has taken on a new meaning for him. Dale respects God and gives honor and glory to God…….for being longsuffering with him. Dale lives with his wife Michele of 17 years, she has been my lover, best friend, business partner, help meet, she is a big inspiration in my life……..and I am grateful God has blessed me with her.